NGOS AND POST-CONFLICT RECOVERY

The Leitana Nehan Women's Development Agency, Bougainville

NGOS AND POST-CONFLICT RECOVERY

The Leitana Nehan Women's Development Agency, Bougainville

HELEN HAKENA, PETER NINNES
AND BERT JENKINS (EDITORS)

ANU

THE AUSTRALIAN NATIONAL UNIVERSITY

E PRESS

Asia Pacific Press at
The Australian National University

ANU

E PRESS

Co-Published by ANU E Press and Asia Pacific Press
The Australian National University
Canberra ACT 0200, Australia
Email: anuepress@anu.edu.au
Web: http://epress.anu.edu.au

National Library of Australia Cataloguing-in-Publication entry

NGOs and Post-conflict recovery: the Leitana Nehan Women's Development Agency,
Bougainville.

Bibliography.
ISBN 0 7315 3745 9
ISBN 1 9209 4218 1 (Online document)

1. Leitana Nehan Women's Development Agency. 2. Non-governmental organizations
- Papua New Guinea - Bougainville Island. 3. Peace-building - Papua New Guinea
- Bougainville Island. 4. Humanitarian assistance - Papua New Guinea - Bougainville
Island. 5. Bougainville Island (Papua New Guinea) - History. I. Hakena, Helen. II.
Ninnes, Peter, 1960- . III. Jenkins, Bert A.

361.77

Editor: Matthew May
Publisher: Asia Pacific Press and ANU E Press
Design: Annie DiNallo Design
Printers: University Printing Service

First edition © 2006 ANU E Press and Asia Pacific Press

CONTENTS

ABBREVIATIONS

AARH	Australian Alliance for Reproductive Health
ABG	Autonomous Bougainville Government
AIDS	Acquired Immune Deficiency Syndrome
AusAID	The Australian Agency for International Development
BACDA	Bougainville Alliance of Community Development Agencies
BCC	Bougainville Constitutional Committee
BEST	Business Enterprise Support Team
BICWF	Bougainville Interchurch Women's Forum
BIG	Bougainville Interim Government
BIPG	Bougainville Interim Provincial Government
BOCBIHP	Bougainville Community Based Integrated Humanitarian Program
BOCIDA	Bougainville Integrated Community Development Agency
BPC	Bougainville People's Congress
BRA	Bougainville Revolutionary Army
BRF	Bougainville Resistance Forces
BTG	Bougainville Transitional Government
BWPF	Bougainville Women for Peace and Freedom
CAA	Community Aid Abroad
CBO	Community-Based Organisation
CDS	Community Development Scheme
CDT	Community Development Training
CEDAW	Convention for the Elimination of All Forms of Discrimination Against Women
CRC	Convention on the Rights of the Child
CWA	Catholic Women's Association
FWCC	Fiji Women's Crisis Centre
IHD	Integral Human Development
INGO	International Non Government Organisation
IWDA	International Women's Development Agency
LCOE	Leitana Council of Elders
LNWDA	Leitana Nehan Women's Development Agency
MDGs	United Nations Millennium Development Goals

NGO	non-government organisation
NZ Aid	New Zealand Development Assistance Program
PCW	Provincial Council of Women
PMG	Peace Monitoring Group
PNG	Papua New Guinea
PNGDF	Papua New Guinea Defence Force
SCF	Save the Children Fund
SCP	Strengthening Communities for Peace
SDA	Seventh Day Adventist
TMG	Truce Monitoring Group
UN	United Nations
UNDP	United Nations Development Program
UNESCO	United Nations Educational, Scientific and Cultural Organisation
UNICEF	United Nations Children's Fund
UNIFEM	United Nations Development Fund for Women
UNOMB	United Nations Observer Mission in Bougainville
VAW	Violence Against Women
VBA	Village birth assistant
WHO	World Health Organisation
WTP	Working Towards Peace
YWCA	Young Women's Christian Association

ACKNOWLEDGMENTS

Peter Ninnes

First of all I wish to thank Helen Hakena for entrusting us with the work of documenting Leitana Nehan's story. It has been a great privilege to work with Helen and her team of staff and volunteers, and to contribute in a small way to their peace-building efforts in Bougainville. I am also grateful to the Leitana Nehan staff and volunteers for their willingness to tell us about their work and share their stories. I hope we have been able to do justice to your courage, commitment and achievements of the last 14 years. I wish to thank the James Blythe Fund, the Faculty of Education, Health and Professional Studies and the University of New England Research Committee for providing funds to support my four field visits to Bougainville to undertake this project. Rebecca Spence, Bert Jenkins and Jonathan Makuwira provided excellent professional support for this project, while Jennifer Chan provided the initial inspiration to undertake work of this kind. I am also grateful to Tamar Doff of the Centre for Research on Education in Context at the University of New England who diligently and expertly proofread the whole manuscript. The staff at Asia Pacific Press, including Maree Tait, Joanne Ridolfi and Matthew May, have been most helpful in compiling the book. Finally, I want to sincerely thank my family, whose support for each other during my absences for fieldwork have directly contributed to the success of this project.

Bert Jenkins

I would like to acknowledge the James Blythe Fund, administered by the Centre for Peace Studies at the University of New England, which funded my first trip to Bougainville in January 2003. I especially thank Rebecca Spence from the Centre for Peace Studies for alerting us to the peace-building work that Helen Hakena and Leitana Nehan were undertaking and graciously giving us contact details to pursue this project. Scott Fisher provided assistance with the first round of interviews in 2003. I am also very grateful to the staff and volunteers of Leitana Nehan for providing information to us. Peter Ninnes also deserves thanks for the oodles of time he spent editing the book and for being so understanding when work commitments slowed the writing process. I also thank my family for allowing me time to work on the chapters on the weekends. Finally, thanks also to Chloe the dog.

1 BOUGAINVILLE FROM CRISIS TO PEACE

Peter Ninnes

Nations in the Southwest Pacific have experienced a number of armed conflicts and episodes of civil unrest in the last two decades. These have included the secessionist war on Bougainville, Papua New Guinea (1988–98), the 'ethnic tension' in Solomon Islands (1998–2003), the three coups in Fiji, the ongoing secessionist movement in Papua, and the occupation and liberation of East Timor (1975–99). In each of these conflicts, grassroots non-government organisations (NGOs) have appeared and attempted to prevent or overcome violence and ameliorate its effects. When government services and control have broken down, or when international NGOs are uninterested or unable to help, grassroots NGOs provide important humanitarian, educational and advocacy services. Yet the crucial role played by grassroots NGOs in conflict and post-conflict recovery in the Southwest Pacific has not been well documented. The aim of this book is to document and analyse the work of one longstanding grassroots non-government organisation based in Bougainville. This NGO, the Leitana Nehan Women's Development Agency (LNWDA or Leitana Nehan), provides many salutary lessons for grassroots NGOs undertaking peace-making and peace-building work. In the 13 years of its existence, it has contributed humanitarian assistance, provided formal and non-formal education programs on peace, gender and development, become a powerful advocate at all levels of society, and expanded its work through strategic partnerships with a host of local, national and international organisations. Its work has been recognised through the award of a UN Millennium Peace Prize in

1

2000 and a Pacific Peace Prize in 2004. This book makes a unique contribution to understanding the role of non-government organisations in promoting peace, gender and development in the Southwest Pacific by recording the story of the Leitana Nehan Women's Development Agency and analysing how it has managed to be successful both during times of conflict and during times of peace. This book shows how the organisation has adapted to changing circumstances in Bougainville, how it has developed and expanded its operations and the impact of these changes on its ability to recruit supporters and partners. The book also analyses the organisation's work in light of contemporary thinking about successful NGOs and effective peace-making and peace-building processes, drawing conclusions relevant to other NGOs undertaking peace and post-conflict recovery work.

The province of Bougainville is politically a part of Papua New Guinea. As a result of the peace process, it has recently gained a high degree of political autonomy. Geographically and culturally, it is part of Solomon Islands (Kabutaulaka 1994), although there are also prehistoric connections to parts of Papua New Guinea (Spriggs 1992). The province comprises the large islands of Bougainville and Buka, a number of small adjacent islands, and the more remote atolls of Nissan, Caterets, Mortlock, Tasman and Fead. Much of Bougainville Island is mountainous, with the highest peaks rising to over 2,000 metres (Oliver 1991), and contains many large rivers, while the southern half of the island has extensive areas of coastal swampland. The climate is tropical, with high annual rainfall.

Archaeological records indicate that Buka has been occupied by humans for at least 28,000 years, with at least one notable further wave of migration occurring 4,000 years ago (Spriggs 1992). Local foundation stories describe the actions of various ancestor figures who created human beings, features of the landscape, cultural and social practices, and various food and artefacts (see for example Blackwood 1979; Oliver 1955).

Bougainville is home to more than twenty languages—members of the Austronesian and Papuan language groups. Tok Pisin, the *lingua franca* of Papua New Guinea, is widely spoken, and English is used as the medium of instruction in all but the earliest years of formal schooling. With the exception of Nissan and Buin, Bougainville societies are matrilineal (Garasu 2002). Thus women in pre-contact times had high social status and a substantial say in community issues, including land use, and land was inherited through the mother's line. Matrilineal systems were disrupted by colonial practices and by the war in Bougainville (Wesley-Smith and Ogan 1992), but they have nevertheless survived.

Ogan (1999) argues that the impact made on Bougainvilleans by European contact, colonialism, the post-colonial era and the Bougainville crisis was varied. Many males from the north of Bougainville Island and from Buka had first contact with Europeans as a result of being recruited as labourers for plantations in Samoa, New Britain, Queensland and Fiji (Oliver 1991). Britain and Germany agreed in 1886 that Bougainville and Buka were part of the sphere of German influence, and they became an official German colony in 1899 (Bennett 2000; Oliver 1991). The Catholic Society of Mary (that is, Marists) established a mission on Bougainville in 1902, followed by a German colonial administration post at Kieta in 1905 (Bennett 2000; Oliver 1991). Plantations began to be established along the coast—resulting in the alienation of land—and the main economic activity of the German colony was copra production. When World War I commenced, the German forces on Bougainville surrendered to an Australian contingent (Bennett 2000), and, after the war, Bougainville, along with other parts of German New Guinea, became a Mandated Territory administered by Australia (Oliver 1991). Wesley-Smith and Ogan (1992) argue that from 1899 up until World War II, Bougainville experienced 'classic colonialism' in which natural resources and labour were exploited, few government services were offered to local people, and missions and planters had more contact with the local population than did government officials.

The Japanese occupied Bougainville from 1942 until the Allies invaded in 1944 (Oliver 1991), exposing Bougainvilleans to the contrasting styles of Americans and Australians. After the war, the contrast between the Australian government's promises and its delivery of government services was just as stark (Wesley-Smith and Ogan 1992). In the two decades following World War II, the Australian government embarked on an era of 'development' in its northern colony, attempting in particular to draw more of Bougainville's population into cash cropping. Bougainvilleans, however, were reluctant to work on plantations, and much labour was brought in from other parts of Papua and New Guinea (Wesley-Smith and Ogan 1992).

The major 'development' event in Bougainville, in terms of social, cultural, economic and political impact, was the establishment of the Panguna copper mine and its associated facilities in the mountains of central Bougainville Island during the last decade of Australian colonial control. According to Oliver (1991), a number of factors combined to make possible the mining of this massive but low-grade deposit: new technology, world demand for copper, entrepreneurial flair, a pro-development Australian government, as well as the establishment of long-term international contracts for the mine products. Exploration, drilling and construction began in 1964, and mining itself commenced in 1972 (Oliver 1991), despite objections from Bougainvilleans (O'Callaghan 2002). The ore body measured about 1 kilometre wide, 1.5 kilometres long and 600 metres deep, and the mine produced millions of tonnes of copper, hundreds of thousands of kilograms of gold and silver, hundreds of millions of kina in taxes and royalties to the PNG government, about 75 million kina in royalties to the North Solomons Province, and 22 million kina in royalties to landowners (Oliver 1991), although the latter royalties were inequitably spread among landowners with primary and secondary land rights (Wesley-Smith and Ogan 1992). The mine provided thousands of jobs, and the mining company provided large-scale training and scholarships (Wesley-Smith and Ogan 1992). However, it also brought widespread social changes (Wesley-Smith and Ogan 1992) and environmental damage (Miriori 2002). The principles of land use employed by the mining company were foreign to Bougainvilleans (Ogan 1999; O'Callaghan 2002), and the mine's operations were the result of legal agreements in which Bougainvilleans had little or no say (Ogan 1999).

In addition to the mine, further context for the years prior to the Bougainville crisis is given by the issue of independence. Ogan (1990) found requests by Bougainville to be administered by the United

States rather than Australia as early as the 1960s. The Hahalis movement in Buka in the 1960s formed in part as a protest against paying colonial taxes, while the Mungkas Association, comprised of Bougainvillean students at UPNG, produced a declaration in 1968 requesting the Australian administration to let Bougainville 'go it alone' (Havini 1990:20). Napidakoe Navitu Association held a referendum in 1971 that they claimed showed that almost 100 per cent of the sample supported independence, while in the same year Paul Lapun, who was involved in the formation of Napidakoe Navitu (Ogan 1999), presented a motion to the PNG House of Assembly for a referendum on Bougainville, but the colonial administration opposed it and it was defeated. The Pangu Pati also proposed a motion to investigate Bougainvilleans' feelings towards the issue but it was also defeated (Havini 1990).

In 1972, the PNG Constitutional Planning Committee examined ways of incorporating Bougainvillean aspirations for independence, leading to the formation of a provincial government system within Papua New Guinea (Ghai and Regan 2002). The deaths of two Bougainvilleans in Papua New Guinea helped to consolidate the independence movement and resulted in the formation of a Bougainville Special Political Committee (Havini 1990; Ghai and Regan 2002). However, negotiations between the Bougainvilleans and the PNG government strained over the issue of financial powers for the province and the perception among Bougainvilleans that there were unacceptable imbalances between national and provincial power and a lack of accountability in the proposals (Havini 1990:22; Ghai and Regan 2002). This led to a unilateral declaration of independence of the Republic of North Solomons on 1 September 1975, sixteen days before Papua New Guinea was due to become independent from Australia (Ghai and Regan 2002; Kabutaulaka 1994). The PNG government suspended the Bougainville provincial government, and, after a year, the Bougainvilleans accepted PNG sovereignty, having gained 'more substantial financial and legislative powers' (Havini 1990:24; Ghai and Regan 2002).

The war in Bougainville had a number of inter-related causes, including a dispute among landholders about royalty payments and concerns about the environmental and social impact of the mine (Claxton 1998; McMillan 1998; Miriori 2002; Ogan 1990; Ona 1990; Regan 1998), as well as the failure of the PNG government and Bougainville Copper Limited to undertake an agreed renegotiation of the mining agreement (Forster 1992). The dispute initially resulted in sabotage against the mine and its associated infrastructure. In response to this sabotage, the PNG government sent in the police riot squad and later the Papua New Guinea Defence Force (PNGDF) to quell the 'criminal' behaviour and protect the nation's economic interests in the mine (Dinnen 1999; Layton, 1992; Namaliu 1990). However, the heavy-handed tactics of these security forces and their abuses of human rights rallied many Bougainvilleans to the side of the rebels, in the form of the Bougainville Revolutionary Army (BRA), and expanded the dispute beyond the issues directly related to the mine (Kabutaulaka 1994; Layton 1992; May 2001; Miriori 2002; Ogan 1990). As a result, older issues, such as autonomy and independence for Bougainville, re-emerged (Ghai and Regan 2002; Hannett 1975; Havini 1990; Ogan 1990, 1999). Mounting casualties and disputes among PNGDF commanders about how to pursue the conflict led to the withdrawal of all PNGDF forces from Bougainville in 1990 (Oliver 1992; Sohia 2002). In addition, many public services and private enterprises, such as banks, withdrew from the province in 1990 as the violence increased (Sohia 2002). Further hardship occurred as the PNG government imposed an economic and communications embargo in mid 1990, resulting in a severe lack of medicine, food and fuel in the BRA controlled areas (Sohia 2002).

Left to rule the province, the BRA commanders and their newly formed civilian government, the Bougainville Interim Government (BIG), had difficulty controlling the BRA's various factions (McMillan 1998; Regan 1998). Violence against Bougainvilleans considered too closely aligned to the PNG government—as, for example, when young people from Inus and Tinputz in north Bougainville Island burnt Ieta village, near Buka (Regan 1998)—resulted in some disaffection with the BRA and the BIG (Regan 1998).

Some areas invited the PNGDF and government services to return, and some groups set up resistance forces to fight the BRA (O'Callaghan

2002; Regan 1998; Sohia 2002). In particular, in September 1990, the PNGDF returned to Buka, where Leitana Nehan began its work. The PNGDF also took control of parts of the north and southwest of Bougainville Island in 1991–92, and, although abuses continued to occur, Regan (1998) argues that PNGDF was more disciplined in this second attempt to control the province.

Up to 50,000 people were placed in 'care centres' in PNGDF-controlled areas, where abuses by the PNGDF were common (McMillan 1998; Saovana-Spriggs 2000). The naval blockade of the island, and particularly the areas controlled by the BRA, meant that essential services such as health and education were shut down, apparently leading to many deaths from diseases that would have been preventable with adequate medical supplies.[1]

Numerous attempts were made to resolve the conflict, with peace talks held on the HMNZS *Endeavour* in 1990, on the MV *Huris* in 1991, in Honiara in 1991 and 1994, at Arawa in 1994, and in Cairns in 1995 (Safu 1992; McMillan 1998; Sohia 2002). However, an effective truce was only signed as a result of two sets of talks at the Burnham army base in New Zealand in 1997 (Tapi 2002; Corry 2002). Several authors attribute the impetus for this truce to the change of PNG government caused by the Sandline crisis (see, for example, Regan 1998; O'Callaghan 2002). A permanent ceasefire was enacted following talks at Lincoln University in New Zealand in 1998 (Regan 1998). A peace agreement was signed in 2001 (Regan 2002a, 2002b), allowing for the disposal of weapons, the development of a constitution for an autonomous Bougainville, and elections for an autonomous government. In early 2005, the Bougainville Interim Provincial Government and the PNG government approved the constitution for an autonomous Bougainville, and elections were held in May–June 2005. At the time of writing, weapons disposal is complete in almost all areas of the province.

Peacekeeping and peace-building in Bougainville have had a number of dimensions. In terms of peacekeeping, the 1997 truce was monitored by a Truce Monitoring Group (TMG), led by New Zealand, and comprising unarmed peacekeepers from New Zealand, Australia, Fiji and Vanuatu. In 1998, the TMG was replaced with a Peace

Monitoring Group, led by Australia. Its task was to facilitate the process of peace-building by monitoring the ceasefire and supervising the collection and containment of weapons (Regan 2001a, 2001b). In July 2003, the Bougainville Transitional Team replaced the PMG.

In terms of peace-building, diverse international actors such as AusAID and the Saika Grassroots Foundation have been responsible for providing funding for the re-establishment of infrastructure, such as new buildings at the Buka Open Campus of the University of Papua New Guinea (Ninnes et al. forthcoming), as well as the construction of roads and wharves. The Bougainville Provincial Government elected in 1999 has been responsible for re-establishing social institutions such as education, health and agriculture, and has worked with a wide range of local, national and international partners, such as governments in Australia, Japan and New Zealand, the PNG government and local churches. In terms of political institutions, autonomous Bougainville's constitution has been developed through a lengthy series of consultations both within Bougainville and with Papua New Guinea (*Papua New Guinea Post Courier*, 17 January 2005). Elections for an autonomous Bougainville government were held in May and June 2005.

Apart from Leitana Nehan, organisations such as the Bougainville Interchurch Women's Forum, the Bougainville Women for Peace and Freedom, the Catholic Women's Association, Bougainville Community-based Integrated Development Agency, Peace Foundation Melanesia, and The Bougainville Trauma Institute are providing a range of relevant services in areas such as critical literacy, reproductive health, small business management, counselling and community development (Böge and Garasu 2004; Garasu 2002; Howley 2003; Saovana-Spriggs 2003; Sirivi and Havini 2004). In addition, church leaders are playing a major role in working with people to undertake reconciliation and conceptualise a new peaceful vision for Bougainville (Fisher 2004). At the same time, many groups are engaging in reconciliation work using methods incorporating local cultural practices of symbolic weapons destruction, exchanges of gifts and religious ceremonies (Howley 2002, 2003; Saovana-Spriggs 2003).

The remainder of this book has two major sections. The first section, comprising Chapters 2–5, describes and explains the history and work of the Leitana Nehan Women's Development Agency. Chapter 2 explores the early lives, schooling and community work of the four founders of Leitana Nehan, as well as the early work of the organisation from its founding in 1992 to its formal establishment in 1994. The chapter shows how the beliefs, values and experiences of life before and during the conflict created the impetus and motivation to form the organisation, how the founders' early work, focused mainly on humanitarian relief, raised their experience in gender-awareness and peace-building efforts and established their credibility in the community. In Chapter 3, we describe and analyse Leitana Nehan's works in its middle phase. During this period (1994–99), the organisation received numerous small grants from international non-government organisations and undertook a range of gender-awareness, peace-building and recovery projects. The chapter identifies the various factors that coalesced to allow the organisation to gain experience in all parts of the funding cycle and establish a track record in project management. The chapter also describes and analyses the political work of Leitana Nehan in terms of organising women and lobbying for peace. The purpose of Chapters 4 and 5 is to describe and explain Leitana Nehan's work in the period 2000–4. During this time, the organisation, in partnership with an Australian NGO, received major funding from an international aid agency for a program called 'Strengthening Communities for Peace'. The chapters describe how Leitana Nehan expanded its efforts to all the districts of Bougainville and recruited and trained teams of volunteers. In addition, the chapter describes and analyses other work undertaken by Leitana Nehan during this period, including education of civil society and government groups and political lobbying, and the impact these have had on communities in Bougainville.

The second section of the book, Chapters 6–8, analyses Leitana Nehan's work through a number of academic lenses. This part of the book is of particular interest to scholars in peace studies, development studies and Pacific island studies. In Chapter 6, Peter Ninnes employs post-structural theoretical frames to explore the ways in which Leitana Nehan has used various discourses of gender, development and peace. He shows the ways these discourses have changed over time to suit the local, regional and global circumstances, and traces the origins of these discourses to diverse sources. The analysis shows the ways in which members of a grassroots NGO have been able to learn and deploy key ideas at crucial moments. In Chapter 7, Jonathan Makuwira explores and analyses the partnerships that Leitana Nehan has entered into, especially the relationship between Leitana Nehan, the International Women's Development Agency (IWDA) and the Australian Agency for International Development (AusAID). The chapter examines the ways in which local and international partnerships contribute to peace-building and post-conflict recovery, and demonstrates the simultaneously complementary and contradictory terrain that global partnerships for peace and development need to negotiate. In Chapter 8, Peter Ninnes reviews Leitana Nehan's work in terms of peace-building, in terms of NGO practices, and in terms of the development of local, national and global networks.

The final chapter provides an epilogue by two of Leitana Nehan's founders, Helen Hakena and Agnes Titus, describing the work that has been done since the end of the Strengthening Communities for Peace project, and reflects on the impact of the work on communities and the volunteers who worked in them.

NOTE

[1]   The number of deaths attributed to the crisis range from 10,000 (Henderson 1999) to 12,000 (Bennett 2000) to 20,000 (Saovana-Spriggs 2000).

2   WE MUST HELP OURSELVES

Peter Ninnes

The Leitana Nehan story begins with three women giving birth on the same day in 1990. These were personal and family crises in the midst of a humanitarian crisis. Helen Hakena, in a speech delivered at the International Women's Day celebrations in Australia in 2003, recalled

> [i]n 1990, when PNG withdrew all services from Bougainville and imposed a total blockade on the island, I was seven months pregnant with my fourth child. Late one afternoon the Bougainville Revolutionary Army chased my husband to our home (in Hahela) after he refused to give them our car. Previously, BRA elements had taken five of our company's vehicles. Kris, my husband, managed to run and hide in the bushes but he had no time to tell me and my three children. We were having dinner in the house and were very surprised to see eleven gunmen come into our home demanding to see my husband. I told them that we didn't know where Kris was, but still they refused to listen, continuing to point guns at me and the children and calling us names, even threatening to shoot us if Kris didn't show up.
>
> The village people found out what was happening and came to our assistance. The gunmen left but the next day they returned in force, beating anyone in their path and destroying homes. Our entire village fled and hid in caves in the cliffs. It was then that I felt labour pains and saw blood. I was also sick with malaria, but we were too scared to leave our hiding place.
>
> My husband sent a runner to get the local doctor as the hospital was closed because of the conflict, and there were no nurses. The doctor persuaded my husband to take me to town. The doctor gave me antimalarial drugs and then, as the hospital was locked, he took me to an old abandoned South Pacific Bank building. It was here, on a bare floor with no light or electricity, and no incubator or oxygen, that I gave birth prematurely to my son Max.

Two other women gave birth in the bank that day. Rena suffered massive blood loss and died ten days after the birth of her son. Maria died from complications caused by a previous caesarean section, although her son survived. After watching these women suffer such tragic deaths, Helen was determined to do all she could to end the violence and deprivation of the war. Ten days after Max was born, however, the entire village where they were staying (Ieta, Helen's husband's village) was burnt to the ground. The family again had to flee to Helen's mother's home, Gogohe, in central Buka. The other residents of Ieta were dispersed all over Buka Island. They were brought to Kubu, just north of Buka town, in November 1990 and placed in a care centre by the PNGDF, following the return of the defence forces to Buka in September of that year.

Even at this early stage of the conflict, many women were becoming victims of sexual assault by combatants. Kris and Helen and their children were the first family to move back into Buka town after the PNGDF returned. As a result, they often hosted other families from various parts of Bougainville who needed somewhere to stay in town. One of the early tasks that Helen undertook to help local women was to advise them to get home before dark after coming to the market. This was to avoid becoming victims of abuse by members of the PNGDF, who would take women away in boats to nearby small islands and rape them. Helen and Kris witnessed two incidents in which women had jumped into the sea to escape. The work took on a more coordinated form in 1992 when Helen's schoolfriend from St Mary's Girls' School in Asitavi, central Bougainville, Agnes Titus, came to Buka from her home on Nissan Island. Agnes stayed at Helen's home, and they discussed the impact of the war on Bougainville women and children. They decided to use the Catholic Women's Association network to find ways to help women and children. This network remained strong despite the war. When Helen was elected Coordinator of the Catholic Women's Association (CWA) in 1992, it had groups operating in 32 parishes throughout Bougainville. The impact of these CWA groups was seen as early as 1990, when the Gogohe CWA, led by Anastasia La Pointe, attempted to organise a peace march to Buka town. The plan was for over 1,000 women to march and air their views about the lack of services caused by the total blockade of the island. The BRA, however, announced that the march would not be possible, and the march organisers were taken to unknown locations where they were verbally abused and threatened. The peace march never took place.

Two other school friends from St Mary's, Alina Longa and Brenda Tohiana, later joined Agnes and Helen. Between the four of them, they had chiefly and denominational connections in most parts of Buka and Nissan. Helen was from Gogoghe on the east central coast of Buka, while her husband Kris was from Ieta in the southeast corner. Agnes was from Nissan; Brenda's home village was Hanahan in the north of Buka, and Alina came from Lemanmanu in the northwest corner of Buka. While each of these founding members of Leitana Nehan had common experiences and connections through the chiefly system, St Mary's school and the CWA, they also brought different life experiences that contributed to Leitana Nehan's initial work. Each had been either President or a member of the student executive at St Mary's. Helen had been a primary school teacher for 15 years before the crisis, while Alina had been a high school home economics teacher in schools throughout Bougainville, including Hutjena High School on Buka, and Buin and Arawa High Schools on Bougainville island itself. Brenda brought experience as an accountant, while Agnes had worked for 16 years as a community development officer for Bougainville Copper Limited, where she gained many insights from her work with women and awareness of the social issues arising from the mine's operations. Agnes also brought to the group some fine-tuned thinking about, and long-standing involvement with, women's issues, having been the founding President of the North Solomons Provincial Women's Council in 1978 and a founder of the North Solomons Women's Investment Corporation in 1980. Along with Elizabeth Cox, Agnes attended the World Women's Forum in Nairobi in 1985, four years before the crisis began.

On the beginning of her own work with women and children during the crisis, Agnes recalls that her international experiences made her realise, 'we can't live with our suffering. We have to help ourselves'. Prior to teaming up with Helen, Agnes had put into practice on Nissan an idea that she had picked up in Nairobi—that, during times of war, maximum effort should be made to maintain services for children. The school in Nissan had been closed as a result of the crisis, so Agnes called a meeting of Nissan women, who, drawing on Agnes's experiences with similar groups in Brisbane, together formed a 'ladies' auxiliary' group which ran the Tungol school on Nissan. Eventually, the ladies' auxiliary managed to recruit two women teachers who continued to operate the school.

Helen also attempted to restore primary education in Lose village, in the Gogohe area. Realising that the many children in the area were growing up without any education, she started a school underneath her house in 1989, which soon attracted children from the nearby villages of Hanpan and Suni. Parents contributed K5 each, and this was used to buy chalk and pieces of masonite to write on. About 30 children attended the school, which Helen taught in from 7am to 10am daily for about a year. In 1990, however, the security situation in Gogohe deteriorated. Soon after the PNGDF arrived in Buka, Helen closed the school and the family moved to Buka town.

One of Helen's early tasks as the newly elected coordinator of the CWA was to organise a meeting of the Buka island CWA groups at Hahela on 8 November 1992. It was as a result of this meeting that Helen and Agnes decided to form the Leitana Nehan Women's Development Agency, with the goal of promoting peace and creating a world safe for women and children. The name was derived from the pre-colonial names for Buka and Nissan respectively, and reflected the early, intended geographical focus of the organisation. This focus was dictated by two factors. First, the security situation at the time restricted movement on the island of Bougainville itself. Second, using the word 'Bougainville' in the name would have been politically difficult, given the divisions that existed in the islands at the time. The organisation did not have a formal motto at first, but later they decided on 'women weaving Bougainville together'. Key supporters of the organisation during its early years, who acted as resource persons, were three of the founders' spouses—Julius Longa, Kris Hakena and Michael Titus—George Lesi, who was the Administrator (that is, head) of the Bougainville provincial civil service, and Father Hendry Saris.[1] The organisation set up office underneath Kris and Helen's home in Buka town, with basic facilities such as a phone/fax and suitable storage space. The latter was important because Leitana Nehan's first major task was to provide humanitarian relief to families in the care centres in Buka. In particular, Leitana Nehan supplied second-hand clothing to these families, which had few or no outside sources of income and were often displaced from their own land and were thus unable even to undertake subsistence farming activities. Through Father Saris, Leitana Nehan was able to link up with Karl Hesse, Archbishop of Rabaul (East New Britain Province), who began sending the organisation bundles of second-hand clothes to be distributed to families in care centres in Hanahan, Hahalis, Gogohe, Kubu, Hahela, Saposa Island and Hon Island. At various times, Leitana Nehan also organised shipments of other materials such as spades, bush knives, mattresses, stretchers and kitchen implements to needy families[2] in Buka and in Paruparu and Morotona on mainland Bougainville. The Red Cross later took over this work.

When the organisation was founded, it was not formally registered as an NGO. The Leitana Nehan founders played a variety of roles in the Provincial Council of Women (PCW) in the early 1990s, and Agnes Titus was elected president of that group in 1994. There were limitations, however, to the activities that could be undertaken as executive members of the PCW, and these caused the founders to establish Leitana Nehan more formally (Chapter 3).

Another early activity of Leitana Nehan involved sending medicine to care centres. Agnes had organised a shipment of medicine to Nissan through Steve Cooper from the Save the Children Fund office in Goroka in the Papua New Guinea highlands. When Helen heard that Steve was coming to Bougainville, she contacted him and arranged for him to send consignments of medicine to Bougainville. The first batch was shipped in metal patrol boxes across the Buka passage to Kokopau on mainland Bougainville, but the shipment was intercepted by the PNGDF and destroyed. When other batches arrived in Buka, it was realised that a more secure method was required to ensure the safe passage of these much-needed supplies. A system was set up in which mothers travelling to the mainland would return with medicine concealed in their baskets, hidden beneath soiled nappies, feminine hygiene products or underwear. Male soldiers from either side of the conflict were very reluctant to poke around in baskets containing such items. They believed that touching such items would lead to premature aging or result in bad luck. In this way, the medicine and clothes were distributed via Kokopau, which is just across the passage from Buka town, and also via Saposa Island off the northwest coast of Bougainville, to various parts of the interior of the mainland.

The relief work in care centres continued through 1993, but in that year Leitana Nehan also began to make contact with outside groups and individuals. Such contact played a major role in Leitana Nehan's development from a relatively *ad hoc* humanitarian relief organisation to a fully-fledged NGO focusing on rehabilitation, reconciliation and development efforts. One very important connection made that year was with Rae Smart, who suggested that Leitana Nehan become an NGO. Rae had worked at the Arawa Technical College until 1989, and knew Agnes through the North Solomons Women's Investment Corporation. In 1993, Leitana Nehan tried to get permission for Rae and a freelance journalist, Sharon Laura, to visit Bougainville, but they were not granted clearance. No outsiders were being allowed into Buka at that time, and even residents of Buka were issued with a red passport when they gained permission to leave the province. Even today, people remark half-seriously that it was when those red passports were issued that Bougainville gained its independence.

In 1994, however, Rae and Sharon did make it to Bougainville. The restriction on outside visitors was temporarily lifted, and they were granted clearance by the then Administrator, the late George Lesi, who later became Assistant Executive Director of Leitana Nehan. At this time, the PNGDF had lifted the blockade of the mainland for a month, which meant that people no longer needed permission from the PNGDF to have large gatherings on Buka. Helen, as coordinator of the CWA, took the opportunity to organise a 'Bougainville Reunion' at Hahela of CWA women from all 32 Bougainville parishes, using funding organised through Julie Eagles from the Australian NGO Community Aid Abroad.[3] Approximately 2000 women came by foot and by boat to the reunion, which was held on 15 August 1994, where they were welcomed and sang songs about their suffering. They were encouraged to pray, talk and negotiate with the parties involved in the conflict to stop the fighting. The reunion was a sign of unity, confidence, courage and determination to move the peace process forward. Sharon and Rae, whose trip was financed by the International Women's Development Agency, documented the experiences of the Bougainville women during the crisis, and made a video of the meeting. They smuggled the video cassettes out of Bougainville taped to their legs, while some other film departed on the same flight, hidden under babies' nappies.

During 1994, Leitana Nehan also started facilitating a range of courses, often in conjunction with the Catholic Women's Association network and Catholic Family Life, with which Alina was involved. These included courses on family life and counselling. The organisation began collecting the names of widows and single mothers created by the war and documenting the atrocities they had faced, including the names and affiliation of perpetrators if these were known. Over 2,000 names were recorded, although a large number of the records were lost when intruders broke into the Leitana Nehan office and stole them. The perpetrators of this theft were never discovered, although military personnel from both sides who had abused women may have felt threatened by the record of these human rights abuses. Not all of the records were stolen, and the remainder were videotaped for safe keeping by Father Malak from the Catholic media organisation in Port Moresby.

Leitana Nehan also assisted 105 women to attend the Catholic Women's Federation conference in Port Moresby from 1–9 September 1994. Helen, in her role as Coordinator of the Bougainville Diocese Catholic Women's Association, managed to arrange transport through an old school friend, Leona Kilo, who was working at the time for the PNG national carrier, Air Niugini.

Flavia Arnold and Elizabeth Andoga, specialists in small income-generating projects and book-keeping from the Business Enterprise Support Team (BEST) in Madang, also visited Buka in 1994. They came to train CWA women, but their training did not have much impact, because the women were still in the midst of the crisis and were not in a position to commence such projects safely.

The Arawa peace talks were held on 10–14 October 1994. Agnes gave the first plenary speech in her role as President of the PCW and declared 'we have not come here to negotiate for peace; we have come to demand it' (Weeks 1994:25). She went on to address her remarks to women on both sides of the conflict.

> I want to talk to my sisters Mrs Ona, Mrs Kabui and Mrs Kauona [the wives of the secessionist leaders] and all sisters and mothers. What you feel, we have felt. The pain of mothers giving birth in the bush—we have felt it. I am a mother and I have children that I love. You are the same. My heart cried when soldiers on both sides were killed. We are mothers; we carried these children. Why must this go on? Give peace a chance. Come out of the bush. Please hear us. All mothers, please hear us (Weeks 1994:25).

During the talks, Agnes also spoke to Joe Kabui by two-way radio and pleaded with him to join the talks under the security of the South Pacific Peace Keeping Force, but he refused (Weeks 1994).

Helen was not able to attend the Arawa peace talks, because she had received two threatening letters as a result of her strong advocacy for peace. Her children had also been threatened. She did, however, arrange for Catholic mothers and children to attend, and they slept under the Hakenas' house in Buka town on their way to Arawa.

The various workshops organised under the auspices of Leitana Nehan became more widespread in 1995. Using K5,000 in funding from the International Women's Development Agency (IWDA), Leitana Nehan was able to organise workshops to raise awareness of alcohol abuse and violence against women, using teams of volunteers that included Francis Botsia, Elizabeth Behis, Yvonne Baito, Leonard Mokela, Bianca Hakena, Audrey Katia, Alina Longa, Helen Hakena and two seminarians, Abel Willie and Chris Rere. These volunteers were paid an allowance of K5 per workshop to cover their expenses (about one US dollar on current exchange rates).

As well as running local workshops, the founders of Leitana Nehan were involved in wider issues concerning women and peace. Alina travelled to Canberra to attend the Bougainville peace talks held on 22 June 1995, and she also attended the National Catholic Women's Conference in Kundiawa, in the PNG highlands. It was in this year, too, that the Fourth Global Conference on Women was held in

Beijing. Agnes had attended the NGO forum associated with the earlier conference in Nairobi, and in 1995 she attended the pre-Beijing preparatory workshop for the South Pacific region, held in Wewak, on the north coast of Papua New Guinea. In September 1995, Helen and Agnes attended the NGO forum associated with the Beijing conference. In many senses this forum represents a key point in the development and direction of Leitana Nehan. Collectively, the founders were increasingly being exposed to a range of ideas and issues concerning women, human rights, peace and humanitarian relief through their own experiences of the conflict, through attending conferences, by being involved with the PCW and the CWA, as a result of support from Community Aid Abroad (CAA) and IWDA, and through early activities such as the Bougainville reunion and the initial awareness workshops. The Beijing forum, however, turned out to be an important catalyst for change in the organisation's identity, focus and means of operation.

IWDA organised funding for Agnes and Helen to go to Beijing. In Beijing, Helen and Agnes felt that the PNG women shunned them at first, but when they heard what it was like in Bougainville, their attitude softened. Even the Bougainville women who had been living behind the blockade and had travelled to Beijing via the Solomon Islands also initially kept their distance. However, Helen and Agnes encouraged all the Bougainville and PNG women to attend each other's sessions and as a result they discovered that they all had a common desire—peace.

For Helen, Beijing was particularly valuable for a number of reasons. She learned from other women in conflict situations about the work they did and how strong they were. She was exposed to wider issues of peace and conflict in other countries, and extended her networks, especially with respect to training, lobbying and solidarity. Helen observed that there were many different groups attending the conference in Beijing who were just doing work for and with women (not men or children). However, Helen and Agnes believed that in Bougainville, families do things together—husbands, wives, uncles, aunties, children; every family member is included. They really wanted to include women, men and children in their work, and they decided that an organisation focusing on, and working only with, women would not be accepted by communities in Bougainville. This is one of the major reasons why Leitana Nehan works with both men and women, has women and men in its executive positions, and women and men in its volunteer teams. The Leitana Nehan founders also recognised that both men and women needed to be part of the efforts to attain and maintain peace in Bougainville. Helen remarked in a recent speech

> [w]e recognise the strong connection between violence against women and the militarisation of Bougainville society. Because of this, Leitana Nehan is working not only with women but also with men, youth and entire communities towards reconciliation and freedom from violence. Building relationships between young people from different communities within Bougainville has been one of our approaches in healing the rifts created by war. We work with ex-combatants and encourage men to be involved in our work to assist their recovery, to 'balance the teams' sharing of experiences' and to involve men in peace-building. 'Hard core' guerrillas are now working with us and talking to communities about the impact of violence on women. They offer powerful role models to other young men in the community. Our anti-violence workshops help boys and young men to understand that the guns and violence of their childhood are not a necessary part of their futures (Hakena 2003:n.p.).

Prior to the Beijing forum, Agnes and Helen did not know much about women's rights and women's issues except what Agnes had picked up on her visit to Nairobi or what they had gleaned from people like Rae Smart. The Beijing forum raised their awareness of concepts and issues concerning human rights. Before Beijing, they had focused on improving family life, living well together as a family and a community, and re-establishing women's traditional leadership role in the family as custodian of the land and resolver of conflicts. The re-establishment of women's roles was at the time (and still is) an important task for Leitana Nehan, because colonialism and the war had severely eroded women's traditional leadership, conflict resolution and custodial roles. However, the women's rights ideas added to and strengthened their ideas about how communities should operate.

When Helen and Agnes returned from Beijing, they discussed the concepts of women's and human rights with people in the parishes on Buka, who agreed that women's rights were compatible with what they needed. As a result, women realised they needed to speak out about their rights because many men were traumatised by the conflict or too intimidated or scared to speak out. For example, two of Helen's uncles were murdered in front of their children because they had spoken out about BRA-instigated killings and disappearances at Hanahan.

Agnes and Helen were driven by concern about the bloodshed and abuses that were occurring during the Bougainville crisis, and their desire for peace and an end to the violence. This motivated them, in the early days of Leitana Nehan, to undertake humanitarian relief for the families in the care centres, and then to expand their work to include organising meetings and awareness workshops using available funds. During these early years, the founders, especially Helen and Agnes, expanded their understanding of women's issues, and began to develop a network of supporters, mentors and allies within Bougainville, Papua New Guinea and in the wider world. The Beijing forum was a pivotal event, and in the next chapter I examine in detail the impact on Leitana Nehan of that event and its expanding work at local, provincial, national and global levels.

NOTES

[1]   A list of Leitana Nehan staff and volunteers for the period 1992–99 is found in Appendix 1.

[2]   Garasu (2002) identifies two other organisations involved in this kind of relief work at various times: the Catholic Women's Association and the Bougainville Community Integrated Development Agency (BOCIDA).

[3]   Garasu (2002) says that the Bougainville Reunion was organised by 'Catholic women' but does not specifically mention Leitana Nehan.

3 PROJECTS, PARTNERS AND POLITICS

Peter Ninnes

As I observed in the previous chapter, attendance at the Beijing forum by two of Leitana Nehan's founders, Helen Hakena and Agnes Titus, had a major impact on the conceptualisation, direction and focus of the organisation's work. In this chapter I describe the formal establishment of Leitana Nehan as an independent NGO. I then examine how it became involved in a number of key peace-building projects, the establishment of a range of important partnerships designed to facilitate the initiation and maintenance of peace, and its ongoing efforts to find a political solution to the Bougainville crisis. This middle period of Leitana Nehan's history, roughly 1995– 99, expanded the founders' experience in managing small to medium-sized projects, a track record that allowed Leitana Nehan to tender successfully for the large projects that have sustained the organisation and its work.

In early 1995, Helen, Alina and Brenda had all been elected to the PCW executive—Alina as vice-president, Helen as secretary, and Brenda as treasurer—but they found that this actually limited the work they could do with Leitana Nehan. The PCW at the time was hierarchical in its decision-making processes, and the president tended to vet all ideas and proposals for action. As a result, the Leitana Nehan founders had difficulty getting funding for the courses and programs they wanted to run. At the same time, they perceived the PCW as being stagnant and wary of involvement in any activities that appeared too 'political'. They also felt that factions in the PCW were threatened by the presence of some of the Leitana Nehan founders on the executive, believing their appointments to be based on political decisions. In fact, Agnes recalled that Brenda and Helen were not invited to any executive meetings for six months at one stage. They tendered their resignations, but Agnes asked them to reconsider and took them to a PCW meeting with the president and a government adviser. Agnes asked the president to reconsider their resignations, but the president refused to do so. Whereas the PCW was unwilling to speak out on women's issues, the Leitana Nehan founders saw many problems arising from the conflict that needed to be addressed. These included addressing violence, abuse by the armed forces, lack of schooling for children, and lack of respect for people's rights, helping young people think about their future, and meeting women's and children's needs. As a result, when Agnes and Helen returned from Beijing, and Alina, Brenda and Helen all resigned from the PCW executive, they began moves to establish Leitana Nehan formally as an NGO by registering it with the Investment Promotions Authority in Port Moresby.

One of the first activities that Leitana Nehan organised after the Beijing conference the 'silent march' in Buka town, timed to coincide with the Bougainville show, which was held in Buka that year.[1] More than 1,000 women participated in protest against the war and the use of rape as a weapon. This march occurred in defiance of the state of emergency in place at the time. The PNGDF stopped the marchers twice, attempting to arrest the march leaders. When asked 'who is your leader?' The women replied 'all of us are leaders. We all own the march'. The soldiers could not arrest all of them, so they arrested no-one. As Helen recounts,

> [w]e knew the prime minister was in Buka [at the time of the march] and the media would be out in force. We walked silently carrying banners we had sewn by hand, with messages of peace. The media saw us and told our story to the rest of Papua New Guinea. Our sisters in Rabaul were so moved by the story that they organised a boat and sailed through the Buka passage, singing peace songs. There was shooting on both sides of the passage before the women arrived. As they sailed though, the shooting stopped. Their singing stopped the guns (Hakena 2003:n.p.).

One of the major roles that Leitana Nehan has played in Bougainville during the last ten years has been to organise gatherings of young people to discuss issues relevant to peace and development on Bougainville, and to help youth deal with the trauma of the war. The first of these youth 'mobilisations' occurred at Gogohe village, on Buka Island, in November 1996 with less than 50 attendees. A similar event was held at Hahela on Buka in early 1997. These two small gatherings turned out to be a trial run for future events. According to Tonissen (2001:33), these mobilisations helped participants understand how violence is 'described, understood and "explained", by men and women separately, in order to examine how [agencies] may develop policies and practices against violence'.

In November 1997 (and following the signing of the truce), Leitana Nehan organised a youth mobilisation using funds supplied by Community Aid Abroad and Oxfam. Although Leitana Nehan had budgeted for 200 attendees, 784 young people showed up, coming mainly from Nissan, Buka, Tinputz, Saposa and Sipai. Fortunately, the Ministry for Bougainville Affairs donated K5,000 towards food and transport costs for the extra delegates. A number of prominent politicians attended the mobilisation, including the Honourable Michael Somare, the Honourable John Momis, the Honourable Michael Laimo, the Honourable Michael Ogio and Joseph Kabui, the Vice-President of the Bougainville Interim Government. The attendees represented all denominations and included combatants from both sides. The meeting was organised through Leitana Nehan's various networks, and its goals were communicated in only vague terms, in order not to alarm the authorities or raise the suspicions of the PNGDF. The meeting lasted five days. On the first day, the organisers encouraged the young people to write stories, songs and poems about life on Bougainville and what they wanted for Bougainville. On the second day, the young people performed songs and dances about their life, particularly during the crisis and in the bush behind the blockade. On the third evening, participants were asked to come and read their poems at the microphone in front of the crowd, moving many of the listeners to tears. Trust was being built—these activities were a way of getting the young people to relate with each other. On the fourth day the participants spent time in groups discussing their fears, and the fifth evening was spent sharing and listening to each other's stories. Each day started with *lotu* (worship), and the program ended with a large church service, focusing on young people's issues, attended by participants and local villagers.

The Leitana Nehan staff were assisted at this first large youth mobilisation by two priests, Father Saris and Father Boniface, as well as Catholic Family Life workers, other church workers, George Lesi, Jessie Walo, Gordon Gunan and Jennifer Hasop. One long-term benefit of this first mobilisation was that Leitana Nehan began recruiting its first volunteers, but the mobilisation also represented a shift in focus for Leitana Nehan. Rather than simply focusing on humanitarian relief work, these mobilisations were a form of peace and community building. As Helen observed in an interview with the *New Internationalist* in 2003,

> [w]e brought young men together with young women to talk about the effects of the blockade and speak openly about the use of rape and guns. The result was a common understanding of each other's fear and a resolve to build awareness among the community (Hakena 2002:n.p.).

A second major youth mobilisation was held in 12–19 November 1999. Again the venue was the Hahela Youth Centre. This time about 2,000 young people attended. The meeting was supported by a K5,000 grant from Community Aid Abroad and Save the Children Fund and K5,000 from the Honourable Michael Somare. The program followed a format similar to the first event, but had more formal input and teaching on topics such as personality integration, gender awareness, women's rights, and alcohol and drug awareness. A third but smaller youth mobilisation was held at Tinputz, on Bougainville Island, in 2000. It was more focused, and was attended by a selection of 88 youth leaders. Topics covered included proposal and report writing, as well as gender and alcohol awareness and human rights training. As was the case with the first major youth mobilisation, the events in 1999 and 2000 turned out to be fertile ground for recruiting volunteers for Leitana Nehan's work.

The personal and professional development that had characterised Helen and Agnes' attendance at the Beijing forum was an early example of the ways Leitana Nehan has used national and international conferences, meetings and workshops to expand its founders' and volunteers' skills, understandings and perceptions. In the mid to late 1990s, Leitana Nehan staff participated in many such events. Alina travelled to Tonga in February 1996 to attend a two-week conflict resolution workshop, and in February 1997 she attended an NGO conference at Vunapope, East New Britain. Three months later she attended the Diocesan Directors' Secretariat Conference in Kavieng, New Ireland, before heading to Sydney for three months for trauma counselling training. In October 1997, Alina attended a conference in Chiang Mai, Thailand, on refugee women in armed conflict situations. The following month she attended the Asia Pacific Development Workshop also held in Chiang Mai. In 1998, Alina attended a three-month course on counselling in drug and alcohol addiction held in Sydney, and in 1999 she spent a month in Australia promoting and explaining Leitana Nehan's work.

Helen was funded by Oxfam New Zealand to undertake counsellor training in Suva, Fiji, in 1996, and in 1997 she attended a review of Community Aid Abroad and Oxfam programs in the Pacific, held at Nymikum, Maprik, in the East Sepik Province of Papua New Guinea. In the same year, Helen attended the Beneath Paradise Pacific Women's documentation project in Suva (funded by IWDA). One outcome of this project was the formation of the Pacific Women Against Violence Network, of which Leitana Nehan remains a member. Helen also attended the international workshop on strategies and services to address gender violence, held in the Philippines. In 1998, Helen and Elizabeth Behis undertook four weeks of counsellor training at the Fiji Women's Crisis Centre in Suva, Fiji, and towards the end of that year Helen attended the Eighth World Council of Churches Assembly in Zimbabwe. Helen's professional development continued in 1999 with a World Vision-funded trip to Melbourne, during which she visited a telephone counselling service, attended the international conference on the use of children as soldiers, participated in a 16-day activism workshop at Ross House in Fitzroy, and attended the international commission of jurists conference at the University of Melbourne. Also in 1999, Helen attended a conference in Malaysia on women in armed conflict situations, funded by the Asian and Pacific Development Centre.

In 1998, Agnes attended the Australian Council for Overseas Aid meeting in Canberra and toured around Australia talking about the crisis, funded by IWDA. Agnes' work for Leitana Nehan, however, was limited during this period because she was also a member of the Bougainville Transitional Government, and had portfolio responsibilities. The fourth founder, Brenda Tohiana, was a founding member of the Buka Urban Council, in which she had been heavily involved since its inception in 1992. However, Brenda had a major role in setting up and managing Leitana Nehan's financial systems and accounts.

Among the other staff and volunteers from this period of time, Francis Botsia, one of the first Leitana Nehan volunteers, attended Integral Human Development training in Goroka in the Papua New Guinea highlands in 1996, and Elizabeth Behis, Francis Botsia and Leonard Mokela attended a similar program in Rabaul in 1997. These events provided training in conducting awareness programs, trainer development programs, and youth mobilisation programs. Francis Botsia and Jessie Walo attended a personality integration and conflict resolution course at Vunapope in 1997, while Bianca Hakena and Elizabeth Behis went to Fiji in 1999 for feminist counselling training at the Fiji Women's Crisis Centre, funded by Oxfam New Zealand. Late in 1999, Bianca and Yvonne Baito also attended a basic computer training course at the Commercial Training College in Lae, Papua New Guinea.

All of these travels were not without risk. The war continued until the truce was signed in 1997, but even after that the culture of violence that had developed and the large number of weapons in the community always posed a threat. As Helen recounted in an address to a symposium at the University of New England in 2003,

[o]n my way to a women's conference in Canberra in 1998 I was held at knifepoint at Port Moresby's Jackson Airport by two unknown persons and told to return to Bougainville. They knew that I was going to attend a conference in Australia where I was going to alert the world about the atrocities inflicted upon the people of Bougainville, especially on women and children. My personal belongings, including the videotapes and conference papers I was to present to the conference, were confiscated. They were returned a day later. I had to return to Bougainville for fear of being sexually abused or killed (Hakena 2003b:n.p.).

In addition to these outside programs, Leitana Nehan facilitated a number of in-house or local staff-training workshops and programs, often run by outsiders. In 1997, Anne David from Oxfam conducted gender training workshops for Leitana Nehan volunteers. Father Makario conducted a trauma-counselling workshop at Hahela, which was attended by Kris Hakena, Helen, Agnes, Brenda, Alina and Delphine Lesi (whose husband was George Lesi). In 1998, Helen Rosenbaum of IWDA conducted a strategic-planning workshop with Leitana Nehan staff. The following year Dr Victor Storm, a senior psychiatrist, director of clinical services at Rozelle Hospital in Sydney, and Chair of the Royal Australian and New Zealand College of Psychiatrists, conducted workshops on mental health issues as part of a visit to Buka and Bougainville to hold consultations with health educators and community leaders. Leitana Nehan organised his visit, with support and advice from the PNG Division of Health. Agnes Titus, Melkio Dare (a nurse from Paruparu) and Aloysius Pukiene (a public health officer) accompanied Dr Storm on his tour, which included two workshops in Buka and others in Arawa and Buin.

During the second half of the 1990s, Leitana Nehan developed and further expanded its work in the provision of workshops and training for local communities. In 1996, Leitana Nehan secured funding from parliamentarian Michael Ogio to send 20 women to the Catholic Women's Conference in Chimbu, in the Papua New Guinea highlands. In the same year, Leitana Nehan also collaborated with the Catholic Family Life organisation to facilitate a personality integration course for Bougainville youth, and ran a community-mapping workshop at Hahela. The latter resulted from a proposal submitted to Oxfam and Community Aid Abroad, which together contributed K8,000 to cover costs. The workshop aimed to help young people identify problems in their communities and the local resources available to solve them. Some chiefs also attended, and the workshop was facilitated by five staff from Community Aid Abroad, including Julie Eagles, Stuart Watson, Anne David, Reiner Tegetmeier and Rebecca Fleisher.

Starting in 1996, Leitana Nehan worked with Theresa Postma from IWDA on a project entitled 'Working Towards Peace'. This program was funded by the AusAID and Non-Government

Organisations Cooperation Program and addressed issues of violence and homebrew abuse (Tonissen 2001) in North Bougainville.

In 1998, Leitana Nehan held the first homebrew and violence against women awareness workshop in Tinputz Primary School, and began assembling its first volunteer team for the Strengthening Communities for Peace project (see Chapter 4). This first team comprised Ezekial Lames, Valentine Tur, Chris Sagolo, Samson Lino, Fabian Kotsin, Norman Tola, Linus Saram, Cecilia Francis and Clement Borats.

The following year, 1999, was an important year in the development of Leitana Nehan's programs and its influence on peace and community-building in Bougainville. The reach of the organisation started to extend beyond Buka and the nearby parts of Bougainville. Awareness programs were held for the first time in the Northwest district of Bougainville (Hahon, Sipai and Kunua). Furthermore, Francis Botsia and Ezekial Lames, Leitana Nehan volunteers who were both former members of the BRA, visited Paruparu in the no-go zone. This area was still controlled by Francis Ona and his troops and generally closed to outsiders. The aim of their visit was to assess recovery needs in the area (see Box 3.1).

A homebrew alcohol awareness program was run in Siwai, South Bougainville in late 1999, one of the 96 such programs run by the organisation that year as part of its Working Towards Peace program, reaching over 10,000 people. The popularity and value of Leitana Nehan's work was demonstrated also by the fact that in June 1999 the organisation held two gender awareness workshops in North Bougainville, funded by the British High Commission, attended by over 400 people. Leitana Nehan also started integrating HIV/AIDS awareness sessions into its programs at about this time, focusing on prevention and operating in an environment in which no reliable data was available about the extent of the disease in Bougainville. In 1999, counselling services continued to be provided, both in the community and in high schools, by which time the organisation had four counsellors—Helen Hakena, Alina Longa, Bianca Hakena and Elizabeth Behis. Most counselling cases concerned rape, domestic violence, sexual harassment or child abuse.

Box 3.1   From BRA to jail to peace-builder *Francis Botsia*

I was in the BRA until 1990, when the chiefs did a reconciliation ceremony between some BRA and the PNGDF. But when I resigned from the BRA, the PNGDF went back on their word and arrested me and sent me to jail in Keravat, in Rabaul, to await trial. I waited for four years in Keravat, except for about nine months when I escaped and was on the run. When I finally came to trial, they decided to hold it in Buka, so they flew me to Buka on the Monday, the trial was on a Wednesday and I was released. The next day the Rabaul volcano erupted and destroyed the town.

I started working with Leitana Nehan after attending one of the youth mobilisations. I was the first president of the Bougainville Youth Association after the crisis. I was appointed at a meeting we had at Gogohe. Then Leitana Nehan started helping me get organised, with assistance from Family Life. I was involved with the youth, and Leitana Nehan helped me with the programs we were running. I saw that the Leitana Nehan programs really helped us, especially the ex-combatants. I got some of the hard-core ex-combatants and took them to the programs, and then we got them to talk to people attending about the impact of the program on them and about our life during the war.

To be honest, the awareness programs really bore a lot of fruit. When we did homebrew awareness we used frogs or we would cut open chickens' intestines and pour pure homebrew on them to show the effect of it. The homebrew would just cook the intestines completely.

I travelled to plenty of places during the crisis. Francis Ona invited us to go through the villages in the no-go zone when we were based in Paruparu. We went through those small villages up around Panguna, along with three women and two male volunteers. There was no access by car. We had to walk from Birempa up to Paruparu, which is quite a long walk. For those of us not used to walking so far, it took from 8 o'clock in the morning and we arrived at Paruparu at 5 o'clock in the evening. We set camp at Paruparu for a couple of days. I had to run a small training for the volunteers to clarify the aims of the program. From Paruparu we had to walk to Chaba river, and from there to Morone, which is up in the Panguna area, then back to Chaba. We did the Violence against Women program, the child abuse program, and the homebrew awareness program. From there we decided to come back from Panguna to Arawa, and we had a chance to catch a vehicle in Panguna or else we would have had to walk another two days to Arawa. Then we caught an Air Sankamap plane back to Buka. Actually we spent three weeks in the whole of the Panguna area, walking to one place, running an awareness workshop at night, sleeping there, then getting up and walking to the next place.

A major new initiative in 1999 was the commencement of Leitana Nehan radio programs on peace and community development through the National Broadcasting Corporation station in Buka. The programs provide information on violence against women, international conventions such as the Convention on the Elimination of All Forms of Discrimination Against Women (CEDAW) and the Convention on the Rights of the Child (CRC), conflict transformation and good governance. Leitana Nehan estimates that the radio programs reached over 10,000 people in Bougainville and nearby Solomon Islands (Hakena 2005). One impact of the radio program in the early days was that people from the no-go zone started to come out to attend awareness workshops. For example, a chief from Bana sent five women to do one of the workshops.

The professional development, peace-building and community development activities described above came about through the generous contributions of a number of organisations and partners. Community Aid Abroad, Oxfam, the International Women's Development Agency (IWDA), the Australian Agency for International Development (AusAID), the Young Men's Christian Association, the New Zealand High Commission and the British High Commission, as well as local politicians and other community and family members all contributed either financially or in other ways to the success of the work being undertaken. For example, in 1999, Kris Hakena's brother, Stan Hakena, who is the Manager of the Keno Foundation, provided new office space for Leitana Nehan at a generous rental rate. Prior to this, the organisation had been in a small galvanised iron clad office in a building behind the City Pharmacy, having moved out from underneath the Hakena's home in Buka town in 1997. Also in 1999, Dr Storm donated an overhead projector, the Division of Health provided a television and video cassette recorder and the British High Commission funded a photocopier.

Further help came from the Truce Monitoring Group, put in place after the signing of the truce in 1998, which provided logistical support for Leitana Nehan's work. Of particular note, however, is the work of IWDA, which first had contact with Leitana Nehan in

1994. In 1997, an IWDA representative, Helen Rosenbaum, developed a constitution and a strategic plan, formalising the existence of Leitana Nehan. Under its new constitution, Leitana Nehan had an executive and a board of directors (see Appendix 4). Helen Hakena became the Executive Director; Brenda, with her background in accounting, became the Financial Officer; while Agnes became the first Chair of the Board. Also in 1998, IWDA and Leitana Nehan jointly devised the Strengthening Communities for Peace project (see Chapters 4 and 5).

A third major focus of Leitana Nehan's work in the second half of the 1990s was political and involved contributing to peace-making at the local, national and international levels. Leitana Nehan was continuing to provide second-hand clothes for families in the care centres, and their reputation in this area led to an interesting encounter with Sam Kauna, military commander of the BRA. In 1996, Sam Kauna called Helen by radio from the no-go zone to ask for clothes for the BRA soldiers to go to the then current round of peace talks. Helen approached the Bougainville Transitional Government for permission, and the government gave her K3,000 with which she bought jeans and other items of clothing. Then Sam Kauna called back and told them how to find them in the bush. A helicopter flew the clothes in to the mountains. It returned loaded with fresh garden produce from the mountains and landed in the PNGDF hospital, which was located near the current Buka hospital site.

Agnes attended discussions about the Bougainville crisis held in Canberra in 1995, but the National Elections in Papua New Guinea in 1997 provided something of a circuit-breaker in the Bougainville crisis—Rabbie Namaliu was defeated, partly as a result of the Sandline crisis (Dorney 1998), and Bill Skate was elected. After the Truce Monitoring Group was formed, Agnes joined a small delegation representing the Bougainville Transitional Government (BTG) which went to Roroinang in the mountains in Central Bougainville to talk with Joseph Kabui, Vice-President of the Bougainville Interim Government (BIG). This was the first time that the BTG had met the BIG face-to-face, and the church in which the meetings took place was full of Bougainville Revolutionary Army (BRA) soldiers.

In 1998, Helen and Agnes accompanied Rarua Skate, wife of new Prime Minister Bill Skate, on a visit to Kurai Village, in the Central District of Bougainville, to meet with women leaders of the Bougainville Revolutionary Army. Although it was a frightening prospect, Helen felt compelled to go, since women in that area remained fearful of travelling. The aim of the visit was to meet face-to-face for the first time and to share experiences from different sides of the crisis. Mainland women at that time viewed Buka women as enemies and sometimes felt that they had not suffered during the crisis simply because they were outside the PNGDF blockade. The meeting in Kurai, however, provided the opportunity to share issues such as lack of social services, high maternal and infant mortality, and abuse by the defence forces. The women listened to each other's stories and realised that they all wanted peace and an end to the war. The mainland women in the meeting comprised many women from the Bougainville Women for Peace and Freedom (BWPF) and the Bougainville Community Based Integrated Humanitarian Program (BOCBIHP), such as Josephine Sirivi, Lucy Madoi, Lucy Sinei and Ruby Mirinika. Josephine Sirivi (1998:57) left a brief account of the meeting, noting

> [a]t this meeting we clearly stated our stand for peace and freedom and our belief for political independence. We discussed how important it is for us to determine our own needs and our preferred ways of implementing development, and we considered the potential for accepting invitations from our sisters in the north to visit them when BIG clearance could determine a suitable future time.

Agnes also visited Canberra in 1997 to address the members of the Truce Monitoring Group (TMG) about the Bougainville crisis, the needs of women and the importance of the TMG being unarmed and including women who could work with Bougainville women affected by the war. In 1999, the MV Doulos visited Buka and Kieta. This nautical bookshop travels around the eastern hemisphere, encouraging young people to read, providing access to a range of Christian and secular reading materials and conducting workshops on spiritual topics. Leitana Nehan promoted the visit among local schools and helped organise a space on shore—a building behind Judith Raban's Guesthouse in Buka town—for the ship's display.

In early October 1999, the Minister for Foreign Affairs and Bougainville Affairs, the Honourable Michael Somare arrived in Buka for continuing discussions on the political future of Bougainville. Relatively few key women leaders were available to attend, their movements still constrained, and many mainland women still held concerns about the consequences of being seen in the presence of such a prominent PNG leader. Helen and Agnes attended the talks, which were held at Hani's Inn in Buka town.

Later the same month, a reconciliation meeting between Bougainville leaders was held on Nissan. Agnes participated in the meeting, as did George Lesi as a member of the Bougainville People's Congress (BPC), having earlier resigned as Provincial Administrator. The resulting 'Nehan Declaration' allowed the Bougainville leaders to negotiate with the PNG National Government to obtain the highest possible levels of autonomy in the short term and a referendum on independence in the long term. This meeting was followed by a round of negotiations between Papua New Guinea and Bougainville leaders in December 1999 at Hutjena United Church on Buka. George Lesi participated as a member of the Bougainville People's Congress. The Hutjena Accord indicated that the main issues for consideration were the issues of autonomy and a referendum, which had been part of the Nehan Declaration signed by Bougainville leaders on Nissan the previous month.

At the local level, a one-day reconciliation ceremony was staged at Hoko, Gogohe, Buka, between Bougainville People's Congress members from Buka and the Leitana Council of Elders (LCOE). This ceremony was necessary because the BPC was comprised mainly of BRA members, while the LCOE consisted primarily of the BRF. The conflict had caused deep divisions. Reconciliation was necessary so that the two groups could work together for peace and recovery. The ceremony was preceded by a number of speeches, including one given by Helen. The ceremony involved, among other things, the members of both bodies stepping over a live pig, walking under an arch of shell money and chewing betel nut together.

Other developments in that year also impacted on the work of Leitana Nehan. In November 1999, the regional member for

Bougainville, The Honourable John Momis, won a court case in which he challenged the legality of the previous suspension of the North Solomon's Provincial Government. As a result, John Momis was reinstalled as Governor of Bougainville in a ceremony held on 29 December 1999, initiated by the Leitana Council of Elders and attended by the President of the Bougainville People's Congress, Joseph Kabui. This ceremony created a further sense of unity among the various factions to the conflict. It also cemented the legitimacy of the BPC government. Both of these events are significant because they created conditions in which Leitana Nehan could further develop and expand its work on Buka and the mainland.

The political work of Leitana Nehan at the local and national levels, and their work on peace and community development among young people came together in a one-day crusade held at Isa beachfront on 23 December 1999. Many young people attended from places such as Tinputz, Sipai, Selau, Kunua/Kereaka and Buka. Bishop Henk Kronenberg was the key speaker at the rally, and there were also speeches by various politicians. This event was important in the expansion of Leitana Nehan's work because it brought together Catholic, Uniting Church and Seventh-Day Adventist youth and leaders in a spirit of unity and a peaceful celebration of Christmas. In some quarters, Catholics had been blamed for the crisis, mainly because the Bougainville Provincial Government had prior to the crisis been composed mainly of Catholics and had been unable to prevent or avert the crisis. Such unity was important to Leitana Nehan, given its strong Catholic roots and its intention to promote peace-building across denominational barriers.

The mid to late 1990s saw Leitana Nehan continue some humanitarian relief work, but the signing of the Burnham peace accord in 1997 and the commencement of the ceasefire in 1998 shifted its work towards peace-building, including community and personal rehabilitation and reconciliation. The 1999 Leitana Nehan annual report estimates that in that year alone the organisation reached nearly 50,000 people through its awareness workshops, radio programs, print media articles and one-off events such as International Women's Day. Nonetheless, the demand for its work far outstretched its various sources of funding, while high travel costs and lack of transport and communication infrastructure also limited the work that could be done. Despite these constraints, during the second half of the 1990s, Leitana Nehan built up an unrivalled track record in program delivery, advocacy and training in Bougainville, leading to funding for major Bougainville-wide programs.

NOTE

[1]   Garasu (2002) relates, '[o]n their return from Beijing, women from northern Bougainville conducted a silent march in protest against the war, in defiance of the State of Emergency'.

4   STRENGTHENING
       COMMUNITIES FOR PEACE

Bert Jenkins

In December 1998, Leitana Nehan developed a proposal for their first
large project for community peace-building on Bougainville, to be funded
by the Australian Agency for International Development (AusAID).
The proposal was revised and resubmitted to AusAID in September
1999 as a project entitled 'Strengthening Communities for Peace' (SCP).
Leitana Nehan was sponsored in this enterprise by the International
Women's Development Agency (IWDA), based in Melbourne, Australia,
with which it had worked in the past (see Chapters 2 and 3), and was to
be a partner in the project. The project was funded as part of AusAID's
Bougainville Reconstruction Program. In accordance with Leitana
Nehan's constitution, the project focused on the organisation's main
goals, namely, to create a less violent and more peaceful Bougainville,
placing specific emphasis on combating violence against women and
promoting women's rights. Phase 1 of the SCP project was funded for
two years, and launched by the Australian High Commissioner, Mr
Nick Warner, on 24 February 2000.

Phase 1 of the project comprised a variety of community-based
peace-building activities, as well as organisational development and
training for Leitana Nehan that provided invaluable capacity-building
for staff and volunteers as project workers and managers. The main
peace-building objective of the SCP project, as outlined in the proposal
(LNWDA and IWDA 1999), was to

> …strengthen the ability of women, communities, community leaders and Leitana
> Nehan trainers to address violence in Bougainville in general and violence against
> women in particular.

Three main areas of peace-building were addressed by the project: reducing direct violence related to alcohol and homebrew consumption; promoting personal development, particularly Integral Human Development (IHD);[1] and providing counselling for those affected by trauma. Peace-building aimed to reduce or eliminate violence against women and families, and raise awareness about human rights, women's rights and the negative consequences of alcohol abuse at both the personal and community levels.

Much of the peace-building work was carried out in such a way that it fulfilled the second objective of the SCP, which was to build the organisational capacity of Leitana Nehan.[2] The fact that Leitana Nehan, with its beginnings as a humanitarian relief operation, had been invited to submit this proposal in 1999 was evidence that major donors and partners considered it ready and able to undertake a major project like SCP. Furthermore, Leitana Nehan proposed to work in partnership with, and under the mentoring guidance of, IWDA, an experienced and well-regarded international women's NGO, with which they had worked successfully in the past. All of the above improved the chances of the SCP project in Bougainville being funded.[3]

In the project proposal, Leitana Nehan provided three reasons why it was an appropriate organisation to carry out the SCP project (LNWDA and IWDA 1999:3). First, Leitana Nehan had already successfully provided a homebrew awareness program funded by AusAID in that donor's NGO Cooperation Program since 1996, also supported by IWDA. This earlier project, 'Working Towards Peace' (WTP), was a forerunner to the SCP project. The SCP project proposed expanding to other parts of Bougainville the awareness workshops conducted successfully under the WTP project, which had focused mainly on homebrew and community violence in Buka, Nissan and Northwest Bougainville. The SCP project also widened the scope of Leitana Nehan's work to promoting awareness about women's rights. This was in addition to addressing the violence against women and families that was directly associated with alcohol abuse and homebrew consumption.

Second, Leitana Nehan argued that it was the right organisation to undertake the SCP project because of its recognition as a successful

NGO, within Bougainville and internationally. It had a favourable reputation as an agency that could deal effectively with women's development issues and thereby play an important role in post-conflict recovery in Bougainville.[4]

A third justification related to Leitana Nehan's ongoing contribution to peace-building through facilitation of healing at the individual, family and community levels, achieved through its earlier awareness programs. A focus on personal healing, personal development and IHD principles was built into the SCP project to cater for people's spiritual needs. The community radio program that had been broadcast weekly across the region by Leitana Nehan since 1999 had already contributed to increasing awareness about the prevalence of violence and social problems in Bougainville. The SCP project was therefore justified as building on strong foundations laid down by Leitana Nehan's earlier programs and projects combatting cultures of violence.

The rationales used for the SCP project provide a clear indication of the need for the project. It dealt with the common problem of residual violence found in many post-conflict societies. Irrespective of whether they were members of the Bougainville Resistance Forces (BRF) or the Bougainville Revolutionary Army (BRA), ex-combatants' purpose in life and very existence for several years had revolved around armed violence. In post-conflict environments, ex-combatants have difficult adjustments to make. Disposal of weapons, for instance, reduces their power; they may find few employment or training opportunities to help them reintegrate into mainstream society, and post-traumatic stress can also hinder re-adjustment to a peaceful society. Under these difficult circumstances ex-combatants may resort to alcohol and drug abuse, which can lead in turn to violence in the domestic sphere, affecting women, children and families. In Bougainville, where a culture of violence remained after the formal cessation of hostilities, the SCP project offered non-violent means through which peace and harmony could be restored in people's lives, paving the way for post-conflict rehabilitation and recovery at the community level.

The SCP project essentially involved training teams of volunteers to undertake peace-building work in communities (see Appendix 2).

Before turning to a detailed account of the project, I first describe three other major support programs and a range of minor activities in which Leitana Nehan was involved. These activities enhanced the organisation's capacity and community exposure, provided valuable support for the SCP teams, and contributed directly and indirectly to the project's success.

SUPPORT PROGRAMS

Three major support programs contributing to Letiana Nehan's peace-building objectives were undertaken simultaneously: a radio program, a counselling service and a theatre troupe. These programs were coordinated predominantly through Leitana Nehan's main office in Buka.

Commencing in 1999, the radio program disseminated information and increased awareness about homebrew, violence against women, and women's rights.[5] The radio program complemented the awareness workshops and other field activities that the teams were busy carrying out across Bougainville. It was a popular program, with anecdotal evidence indicating that many people listened on a weekly basis. It served to highlight the work being conducted by the teams at various localities and thus helped to reduce violence in many communities. It also promoted communication between local communities and the field teams about social problems that needed urgent attention (see Appendix 5).

The counselling service provided not just counselling but also basic legal advice to victims of rape, incest and domestic violence, with the aim of empowering women to move out of abusive domestic situations where necessary. A handful of counsellors associated with the organisation had sufficient training to undertake this difficult task. As noted earlier, Helen Hakena, Bianca Hakena and Elizabeth Behis had attended training programs in basic counselling, feminist counselling and legal literacy at the Fiji Women's Crisis Centre, while Alina Longa, one of the Leitana Nehan founders who worked for Catholic Family Life, also provided counselling services. However, they were all based in Buka and worked mainly at the Leitana Nehan office, where renovations had been made to accommodate counselling in a private space designed for this purpose.

Leitana Nehan had planned initially for counsellors to spend up to eight weeks per year travelling to various parts of Bougainville to offer counselling services to women in the more remote areas. It turned out that it was not feasible or efficient for occasional trips by trained counsellors from Buka to meet the regular demands for counselling faced by the field teams. The fact that counsellors were expected to produce monthly counselling records and three-monthly data reports indicates the planned frequency of activity. Regular visits were not a practical or viable proposition under the circumstances in Bougainville, especially because of high transport costs, which would have strained the budget, and other substantial communication constraints (LNWDA 2000a). It was necessary, therefore, to train counsellors who could work in the districts alongside the teams.[6] These mobile field counsellors kept records, helped people as much as they were able and identified people who needed advanced counselling, whom they referred to the central counselling facility at the Leitana Nehan office in Buka. The team counsellors identified individuals and families that needed counselling and/or legal support and reported these needs to the Leitana Nehan office in Buka for action by the more experienced counsellors based there. It was expected that counselling statistics and records would be used to plan Leitana Nehan's media and community awareness activities, and also to lobby for policy reforms and improved services for women and families that needed special attention during the trauma-influenced post-conflict period. Nevertheless, it was difficult to expect immediate attention to demands for government action and policy changes in a situation in Bougainville where governance was a complex combination of provincial, local and PNG administration.

Leitana Nehan staff members were aware that counselling was not something that Leitana Nehan could or should carry out on its own (LNWDA and IWDA 1999), at least partly because the organisation had only a few counsellors sufficiently trained to carry out the work. According to the proposal, the teams would not be specifically involved in trauma counselling themselves but team members were to be trained as informed fieldworkers who understood the context and sensitivities surrounding their activities in relation to post-traumatic stress and how this had affected both individuals and communities following the conflict.

Counselling was required for males as well as females. In one case, for example, a boy had been mute for seven years as a result of witnessing attacks on his relatives. Helen counselled him that it was not his fault; he was only very young at the time of the attacks, and he did not have power to stop it. Then he burst out crying and spoke for the first time since the attacks, saying it was true; he had blamed himself for not being able to help them. He said that if he had been bigger, he would have killed the attackers.

By the end of Phase 1 of the SCP project, Leitana Nehan was aware that the demand for counselling at the community level was greater than anticipated. Although many social problems were identified during SCP 1, meeting this demand for counselling was largely beyond the scope of the project; more funds were needed to train a number of field-based counsellors to address the many and varied social problems that existed in the communities. Leitana Nehan realised that the counselling skills that were called for in the communities were more than IHD alone could address.

The Hihatuts Theatre Troupe played a key role in supporting the field teams by reinforcing the messages broadcast on the radio and through the print media regarding social problems and violence in communities. They did this creatively through village or street theatre. Hihatuts specifically assisted Leitana Nehan in increasing awareness about highly sensitive issues relating to rape, incest and domestic violence, which were commonplace in some communities but too confronting to address directly. Some community leaders were reportedly reluctant to allow Leitana Nehan to conduct workshops because of the possibility that they would raise very sensitive issues and expose, inadvertently or otherwise, the individuals responsible, prompting greater community instability. In these difficult circumstances, the troupe was instrumental in drawing victims of violence into dialogue with team leaders and Leitana Nehan counsellors, thereby enabling the teams and community representatives to deal with these problems sensitively or alert authorities when and where it was appropriate to do so.

OTHER ACTIVITIES

On 6–8 March 2000, Leitana Nehan organised International Women's Day celebrations, which also involved a peace march by 300 women in Buka.[7] Two days prior to this, Leitana Nehan held a workshop on violence against women, attended by many women from all over Bougainville, where they discussed gender issues, safe motherhood and HIV/AIDS (LNWDA n.d.).

Leitana Nehan organised a multi-sector workshop for NGOs working in Bougainville and the rest of Papua New Guinea at the end of May 2000 to discuss development needs in the region (LNWDA n.d.). This event shows how Leitana Nehan was increasingly taking the lead in organising development strategies with other NGOs in the region.

At the end of June 2000, Community Aid Abroad/Oxfam Australia visited Leitana Nehan to strengthen their relationship with the

---

Box 4.1   Dramatic experiences for the Hihatuts Theatre Troupe
Fabian Kotsin

The reason we started the theatre group was because of illiteracy. Plenty of kids missed out on school and didn't understand issues in the awareness program. So we decided to make a theatre group to make it easier to communicate with these youth who were illiterate. It was easier to communicate the ideas using actions, especially when they don't speak *tok pisin*.

I am the director of Hihatuts, and I was the founder. The other founders were Ezekial Lames and Quentin Hotsia. One time we went up to Wagog, in Tinputz district. We were doing the awareness program and a boy stood up and he said, 'these people are lying to you. I am a frog, I can drink. I can prove it by drinking this bottle!' He had a 350ml Coke bottle of pure homebrew, and he started to drink it. When he had drunk half of it, he collapsed. They took him to the hospital in Tinputz but the PNG doctor said they had no treatment for alcohol poisoning, so they set off for the hospital in Buka, but he died on the way.

Another time we performed at a place on the other side at Kokopau, They were having games and we went to entertain them. Then we started performing one of our plays. In the play, I started to sing about children and women, and the kinds of violence they experience at home. The song is actually about children's rights. The crowd was so moved by this song, called 'the dream', that by the time I finished, many people in the crowd were in tears.

organisation and plan a youth development project (LNWDA n.d.). The visit led to a project, subsequently funded by CAA, to run youth development workshops in Bougainville, the first of which—on Youth Capacity Building—was held in Buka in August 2000 (LNWDA 2001a:8–9). Thirty young people attended the workshop, which was based on the premise that youth empowerment is the key to youth development (LNWDA 2001a:9). The main purpose of this training was to prepare young people to work more effectively in organisations and to provide them with basic management and organisational skills. The organisational development skills learned at the workshop were essential for young people who were interested in working for an NGO or setting up community-based organisations (CBOs). As Buka became the administrative centre in Bougainville during and following the crisis, many people including youth had moved there in the hope of gaining employment. All of the topics covered during the training in Buka were relevant in the context of developing and administering CBOs in rural areas.[8] The establishment of CBOs later became one of the objectives of SCP Phase 2, under the umbrella of community development and particularly organisational development. A monitoring and evaluation exercise carried out by project officers at a one-day workshop in Buka in November 2000 determined that 90 per cent of the young people who had participated in the August training session were applying the skills they had learned in their respective workplaces (LNWDA 2001a:9).

Apart from establishing the SCP project in 2000, Leitana Nehan was simultaneously supporting the establishment of other women's organisations on Bougainville. For example, Agnes Titus, with funding and training support from Helen Rosenbaum and Annie Goldflam from IWDA, organised and ran a capacity-building workshop for the Siwai District Women's Council (LNWDA 2001a:12). The workshop was held in Tonu in the south of Bougainville from 28 September–6 October 2000. The workshop aimed to facilitate strategic planning, which involved developing a vision and strategic plan as well as furthering the understanding of organisational roles and responsibilities. It also sought to develop organisational programming skills with respect to project planning, implementation and management, as well as monitoring and reporting.

This approach to community development demonstrates Leitana Nehan's mentoring and facilitation role in support of the organisational development of a women's CBO in the far south of Bougainville, far removed from the administrative centre in Buka. Leitana Nehan's contact in Siwai was Anne Rangai, who was also a graduate of Asitavi High School, and who was the informal coordinator of women's activities in the Siwai district administration. When Agnes and her team arrived to conduct the workshop, they found a circular from the Minister of Women's Affairs of the Bougainville Interim Provincial Government, ordering district officials to cease all involvement with Leitana Nehan on the grounds that the BIPG had not been officially informed of the workshop. District officials, however, had been informed and approved of the workshop, so the Leitana Nehan team ignored the BIPG directive and went ahead with their program. The women who participated so appreciated the workshop that they gave each of the presenters six pieces of the basketware for which the area is famous (so-called Buka-ware) as gifts, and even sent other gifts at a later date. This example of a liaison with a women's organisation in the south later helped Leitana Nehan in extending its work through SCP in a part of Bougainville more remote from its centre of influence in the north.

The second workshop for youth, funded by CAA, was held in Tinputz from 3–8 December 2000. It focused on 'youth mobilisation' and was attended by 83 people, of whom 63 were youth (LNWDA 2001a:9–10). The aims of the Tinputz youth training were somewhat different to those for the Buka training in that they concentrated more on peace-building and conflict transformation, particularly establishing, reorganising and strengthening the young people's work; bringing young people together as a means of promoting peace, unity and reconciliation; empowering young people to identify the roles they could play in rebuilding their lives in Bougainville, in a post-conflict situation; encouraging young people to understand fully the importance of their cultural heritage; and guiding young people to access the information they needed to pursue their own personal enrichment.

The Tinputz workshop demonstrated a need in the district for young people to reflect on, and learn about, peace and reconciliation following the crisis, since during that time there had been much conflict between groups of youth affiliated with either the Bougainville Revolutionary Army or the Bougainville Resistance Forces in the area. The workshop enabled young people to express their views about issues affecting the peace process and development in Bougainville (LNWDA 2001a:10). The subjects covered during the workshop included personal relationships, gender awareness, family life, trauma counselling, HIV/AIDS awareness, community policing, the role of the Peace Monitoring Group (PMG), and youth participation in peace-building and development projects (LNWDA 2001a:10). It is obvious that many of these topics are directly relevant to the SCP project and the general objectives of reducing violence in society and violence against women. From a different perspective, both the youth training programs in Buka and Tinputz were aimed at getting young people to consider how to rebuild their lives constructively. The more destructive paths that young people could follow in post-conflict Bougainville included formation into groups that instigated violence and crime or engaged in illegal activities such as the brewing and drinking of alcohol, which in turn could lead to violence or crime. The youth workshops demonstrated constructive pathways for young people as alternatives to crime and violence.

At the same time as the SCP project was getting off the ground in 2000, Leitana Nehan was involved in a number of projects associated with peace-building agendas that involved awareness training workshops, meetings and advocacy, especially in relation to gender awareness and women's rights (LNWDA 2001a:10).[9] Apart from AusAID funding for the SCP project, in 2000 Leitana Nehan obtained over K95,000 in funding for a range of small projects, from donors including the PNG Community Development Scheme, CAA Oxfam, the New Zealand High Commission, IWDA and the Asian and Pacific Development Centre (LNWDA 2001a).

In 2001, Leitana Nehan continued its role of supporting other women's organisations, even though a large proportion of its time was devoted to the implementation of SCP Phase 1. Helen Hakena and George Lesi ran a capacity-building workshop in Buka, which was attended by 20 women and focused on the organisation and management of a CBO (LNWDA 2002a). The women received training in project management, project planning and meeting procedures. George Lesi and Agnes Titus later repeated the workshop on Nissan for women's organisations on the atolls.

Besides its facilitation role in empowering other women's organisations, Leitana Nehan was involved in training people in the area of women's health. For instance, Leitana Nehan organised a training course on 'village birth attendance' from the 10–22 September 2001 for 46 women. The course, funded by the Australian Alliance for Reproductive Health (AARH), was conducted by Aloysius Pukiene and Maggie Kenyon (from AARH) and aimed to reduce the number of mothers and children dying during childbirth, a major problem in Bougainville.

Some of Leitana Nehan's activities were not at all related to donor-funded projects. For example, in September 2000 Leitana Nehan was instrumental in organising and participating in a march organised by the Buka District Council of Women to muster public support for the peace process. The women specifically asked for an ongoing commitment to the ceasefire and Buin peace declaration; the leaders in Bougainville and Papua New Guinea to continue negotiating to reach a lasting peace agreement; the protection of private and public property; and a policy of zero tolerance for any form of violence (LNWDA n.d.). The women presented a petition in support of the peace process to Governor John Momis, who represented the Bougainville Interim Provincial Government, and to the President of the Bougainville People's Congress, Joseph Kabui. In this way, Leitana Nehan was active in advocacy and in empowering women to influence the peace process in a positive way. The women's march on 13 September followed the sixth political negotiations for peace between the PNG national government and Bougainville leaders. The negotiations took place in Rabaul between 4–6 September 2000 to discuss details about autonomy for Bougainville, the referendum for independence and arms disposal.

On 23 December 2000, Leitana Nehan was notified that it had been selected as a winner of the Millennium Peace Prize for Women. This joint initiative of the United Nations Development Fund for Women (UNIFEM) and International Alert (LNWDA 2001a) awarded three prizes to individuals and three to organisations. The cash component of the prize was placed in a UNIFEM account to be accessed by women's groups around the world. The prize was international recognition for the peace work that Leitana Nehan had carried out. Helen, Brenda Tohiana, Celine Kiroha and Anne Harepa travelled to New York in March 2001 to receive the award. On the morning of the award ceremony, Helen was surprised to receive a telephone call from UNIFEM, asking her to represent the women of the world in delivering to UN Assistant Secretary General Angela King a petition containing 350,000 signatures calling for greater participation by women in all peace-building processes.

In addition to the activities described above, the leadership of Leitana Nehan, including Helen as executive director and George as deputy executive director, contributed in a number of other ways to improving the profile of the organisation in the period 2000–04 when the SCP project was underway. Helen travelled widely to promote Leitana Nehan and to learn about peace issues in the international arena of post-conflict peace-building. In October 2000, she attended a peace symposium at Parliament House in Canberra, Australia and a workshop at the Australian National University on 'Conflict and Peacemaking in the Pacific' (LNWDA n.d.). Helen returned to Australia in April 2001 to attend a 'Small Arms and Conflict' workshop held in Brisbane. In July 2001, Helen spoke at the United Nations in New York on the suffering of women in conflict and post-conflict situations and at the UN conference on 'Illicit Trade in Small Arms and Light Weapons' (LNWDA 2002a).

Helen Hakena is also an accomplished facilitator and trainer. She is often called on to act in this role for Leitana Nehan and other organisations. For instance, Helen conducted training for police personnel in September 2001 on the topics of gender awareness and basic counselling to help them develop appropriate skills when dealing with clients (LNWDA 2002a).[10] This approach to training personnel in government agencies was expanded further in Phase 2 of SCP.

Helen also underwent leadership training and professional development by joining women leaders in peace-building at different training conferences. For example, in November 2001 she attended the

'Facilitation and Conflict Transformation' workshop in Fiji, which was run by the Eastern Mennonite University from the United States. She also participated in the 'Women Peacemakers Program', which was organised by the International Fellowship Of Reconciliation. She participated in one such workshop in Oxford in 2002 and a second workshop, on the adoption of 'non-violent conflict resolution' strategies, in Timor Leste in 2004 (Hakena 2004).

George Lesi was the deputy director of Leitana Nehan during the SCP project. He had been the Chief Administrator of the Bougainville province of Papua New Guinea and hence was well versed in the areas of governance, organisational development, project management, project design and project programming as well as monitoring, evaluation and reporting. George was also called upon to conduct workshops or to review programs in organisations other than Leitana Nehan. In 2001, for example, he conducted a review for the Rabaul Archdiocese and facilitated capacity-building workshops for the AusAID-funded Community Development Scheme (CDS) in three provinces of Papua New Guinea.

Other Leitana Nehan staff and volunteers were also involved in a range of activities outside of the formal confines of SCP Phase 1. As noted earlier, Leitana Nehan was a founding member of the Pacific Violence Against Women Network. They continued their involvement during this period of their history by sending Agnes Titus and Fabian Kotsin to Pacific Violence Against Women Network workshops in Fiji in 2001.

SCP PHASE 1 PROJECT DESIGN AND ORGANISATION

The SCP project involved selecting and deploying 10 teams of volunteers to conduct community awareness workshops in the areas of homebrew, violence prevention and IHD. Each team initially had five members, including a team leader and four project volunteers. At least one or more of these volunteers were women. Team members were selected on the basis of their willingness, experience and skills. Members received a *per diem* payment for their work only when they were engaged in an activity with a local community group or involved in training or reporting. The plan was to deploy eight teams on the main island of Bougainville, one team on the island of Buka, and another team on Nissan and nearby atolls. Two project officers coordinated team activities. Andrew Goman was originally responsible for the teams the North (Nissan, Buka, Selau/Suir, Tinputz and Northwest), and later this responsibility was assumed by Hilary Laris, and then Rose Trongat. Rose had taught Agnes, Helen, Brenda and Alina at Asitavi High School, was later employed to cover IHD training for volunteers and community representatives. Benedicta Noneng was the project officer responsible for teams in the South and Central parts of Bougainville (based in Wakunai, Paruparu, Buin, Siwai, and Bana). As the work developed, Benedicta became responsible for the teams in the central area, while Anne Rangai coordinated the teams in the south.

Each project officer had specific administrative tasks within Leitana Nehan. They were responsible for organising workshops for the teams and leaders, coordinating volunteer trainers for workshops, reporting on project activities and producing field manuals. They were also involved in producing support materials and providing advice and general support for the teams. However, the project officer responsible for the teams in South Bougainville, Anne Rangai, was later trained as a counsellor in Fiji and hence had dual roles to play in her interactions with the teams and volunteers. Anne's training in counselling made sense because of the isolation of these districts from Buka, where the other counsellors were based.

The project concentrated on three major activities and three support programs in relation to the primary objective of building peace at the community level (LNWDA and IWDA 1999).

PROJECT ACTIVITIES

Awareness workshops on homebrew and violence

Awareness workshops were conducted for over 120 community groups, including schools, spread over the main island of Bougainville, the island of Buka, and on Nissan and the other atolls. The workshops aimed to increase awareness of health and community effects of homebrew alcohol and its links to violence in the community. The types of violence addressed included various community disputes and family problems (marital problems, rape, incest, child abuse and financial difficulties). Discussions during an initial one-day community workshop identified key issues for each community and prompted the community to hold further meetings to address their own social problems. This process increased the number of participants in follow-up workshops carried out by the teams to target the issues identified by the communities. In addition, the teams encouraged communities to formulate their own solutions to local problems. In many cases, the workshops, meetings and discussions helped local communities develop strategies that would reduce alcohol-related violence and other social problems, and reduce the production and consumption of homebrew.

The awareness workshops were linked to the IHD workshops described below under the second major activity of the project, in which a number of volunteer 'community representatives' were trained to work in their own communities. These community representatives functioned as a link between Leitana Nehan field-teams and members of each community. The local communities were involved in selecting their community representatives using criteria developed by Leitana Nehan. The teams assisted with this selection process during or soon after the initial awareness workshop. The teams trained community representatives in how to engage with their own people in raising awareness about social problems; organise gatherings to discuss issues; identify individuals who need counselling; and devise strategies to reduce violence in the community. The follow-up workshops concentrated on fine-tuning local strategies for violence prevention with local input from the community representatives. By working together they were able to try new initiatives and monitor changes in behaviour and record incidents of violence between workshops, thereby catering for the specific needs of each community.

Community representatives played an important role in developing strategies to end violence at a local level. The field teams supported their endeavours to address the root causes of social problems that had led to local conflicts. In addition, the teams planned to organise the community representatives into a network as a means of empowering them to support each other. However, despite their best intentions, the teams were not in any position to train the community representatives beyond basic empowerment and facilitation functions. The community representatives needed more training to carry out the work that the teams had commenced in their local communities. This was difficult to achieve without additional funding. Furthermore, the teams would have had to spend a lot more time in the districts if they were to reach every village on Bougainville in ongoing workshops. Such coverage was beyond the scope of SCP.

Training in IHD techniques for the community representatives

IHD workshops were planned in order to train the volunteers and community representatives in a very basic form of counselling. Community representatives were trained in the essentials of applying IHD at an intensive workshop that followed the initial awareness workshops in communities. The aim of this activity was to establish a network of local community representatives who could support each other to be effective in their respective communities beyond the life of the project. They were trained to apply IHD principles in addressing violence and social problems through the avenues of personal development and individual healing (Byrne 1983). Leitana Nehan readily acknowledged their Roman Catholic influence (see also Chapter 6). Therefore, IHD was the accepted grassroots vehicle of the SCP project in the bid to eliminate violence at the local community level in Bougainville. In the project proposal, Leitana Nehan and IWDA (1999:10) provided the following description of IHD workshops for training community representatives.

The IHD workshops would explore the wide range of factors that cause violence and disharmony in the community, including anger, grief, fear, trauma, and lack of self understanding, lack of self worth and insufficient guidance/direction for young people. Through analysis and reflection, the workshops aimed to equip the community representatives with the tools to facilitate psychological, emotional and spiritual rehabilitation, and to motivate communities to address their social problems creatively.

Community representatives who participated in IHD training went on to plan and conduct IHD meetings for community groups as well as one-on-one IHD counselling sessions with individuals to help resolve social problems and reduce violence. This was not as effective as having fully trained field counsellors but it was the best that could be done at the time. The community representatives' main role was to empower communities to work at identifying and analysing their social problems, and mobilise them to develop strategies that would reduce the incidence of violence. It was hoped that this process would lead to the resolution of local conflicts and build social cohesion, thereby reducing the chance of further violence in society. The community representatives were encouraged to work together by holding joint workshops, sharing information and experiences and debriefing each other, strengthening their collective efforts through networking. These unpaid volunteer community representatives were perhaps the most important players involved in local grassroots peace-building. The Leitana Nehan field teams facilitated their local efforts and wherever possible provided limited capacity-building. Apart from this, they had to depend on their local networks and basic training in IHD. The project officer employed in the second year of Phase 1 specifically concentrated on training volunteers and community representatives in IHD as well as providing training and support for IHD in the 10 districts. The question remains whether IHD by itself was sufficient to deal with the social problems that the teams uncovered and experienced in communities across Bougainville.

Training of trainers workshops for teams

The teams of Leitana Nehan volunteers were trained during three training-of-trainers workshops conducted at different stages of the project to coincide with the community awareness workshops, the initial workshop and consecutive follow-up workshops. This training process was timed to prepare teams prior to their work in the villages and schools and to incorporate changes based on lessons learned when planning subsequent activities. Thus the training-of-trainers workshops provided invaluable preparation for planned field activities. Each workshop ran for two weeks. More time, however, was spent on training team leaders than on training other team members. The first week of a training-of-trainers workshop was generally devoted to engaging only with team leaders and their assistants, while entire teams were present in the second week.

The training-of-trainers workshops aimed to train the 10 teams to carry out planned activities with community groups. These activities included the initial awareness workshop, up to two follow-up workshops, and various other interactions with community representatives and local leaders. The training-of-trainers workshops involved 10 team leaders and 40 volunteer assistants in Phase 1. Training in the workshops focused on the main activities of violence reduction and IHD. Participants were trained to provide useful follow up support to community representatives, monitor local activities and report on outcomes and lessons learned. They were trained in gathering feedback on the impacts of each workshop, collating information about each community and situation, and collecting and recording information for reports that project officers and the directors compiled for the donor and mentor agencies. The workshops were also intended to gather information to produce a training manual to aid teams in their field activities. The manual was updated over the duration of the project as new experiences and understandings informed the teams' practice.

Community development skills were addressed in the workshops to enhance effective interactions with community groups. The workshops prepared team leaders and volunteers to organise and conduct workshops, make confident presentations to community groups, and trained them in ways to approach, consult and liaise with community leaders. They were also trained in motivating community groups to develop local strategies, reduce violence and act decisively in addressing their social problems. In addition, they were trained to work efficiently in teams. For example, the teams were trained in how to include women in active roles and how to facilitate discussions on sensitive or contentious issues when these matters arose.

Specific topics covered in the workshops included IHD, gender analysis and equity, homebrew awareness, violence against women, women's rights, children's rights and conflict resolution (LNWDA and IWDA 1999). Experienced local trainers were selected to conduct the workshops. Accordingly, the workshops covered different aspects including drug and alcohol abuse, HIV, family life issues, trauma and IHD counselling (LNWDA and IWDA 1999). A workshop was carried out in May 2000 (LNWDA 2000b) at the beginning of SCP Phase 1, and another refresher course was conducted in April 2001 for team leaders and one assistant from each team (LNWDA and IWDA 2001; LNWDA 2002b). In addition, basic training was provided to team leaders at a strategic planning workshop in the first quarter of 2000, which was at the very beginning of Phase 1 SCP. The project officers were responsible for organising the workshops in SCP.

CHALLENGES ENCOUNTERED IN THE SCP PROJECT

At a time of great risk and scarce resources, Leitana Nehan was one of the few active local organisations during the Bougainville crisis, but most of their efforts were restricted initially to working with people in the care centres in PNG government controlled areas (see Chapter 2). During the same period, another organisation, the Bougainville Community Based Integrated Humanitarian Program (BOCBIHP), had begun operating in a similar capacity[11] in areas that were not controlled by the PNG government. In order to expand their work in SCP 1 to other parts of Bougainville, Leitana Nehan initially had to broker an agreement to work together with BOCBIHP (LNWDA and IWDA 1999). This agreement was possible and widely supported in the northeast, south and central parts of Bougainville as a result of visits to the no-go zone made by Leitana Nehan team leaders and ex-BRA operatives Ezekial Lames and Francis Botsia in 1999. A subsequent agreement to carry out the SCP project in the central parts of Bougainville enabled Leitana Nehan to recruit project staff and volunteers from these localities and others in the central district where the BRA had more influence on local people during and soon after the conflict. Leitana Nehan faced a major challenge in extending their work from the north, where they had considerable influence, to cover the whole of Bougainville. It is therefore not surprising that the pace with which the organisation could implement its programs varied across districts.

Access into communities was usually straightforward for Leitana

Nehan in the central, southern and western districts. In a very few cases, chiefs or other organisations carrying out humanitarian work or community development were initially reluctant to support Leitana Nehan's work. In these situations, community members and the people who could see a need for the work that the teams were proposing would invite them into the community, accommodate them and feed them. In most of these cases, the community leaders and the other organisations eventually came around to seeing Leitana Nehan's work as important and relevant. For example, Leitana Nehan received an invitation to work in Gohi village, even though another NGO was working in the area. As a result of one of the youth mobilisations at Hahela, attended by Gregory Manau, the former BRA commander in Tinputz, and Francis Kera, another ex-BRA member, Leitana Nehan was invited into the Tinputz area. Gregory and Francis later became Leitana Nehan volunteers and helped implement the work in that area.

There were seven teams present at the initial strategic planning workshops conducted during Phase 1 of SCP in April 2000. A team from the northwest, Kunua/Kereaka, attended the first training-of-trainers workshop in May 2000 but was replaced later by a collective northwest team. The initial eight district teams in SCP Phase 1 were from Nissan, Buka, Selau/Suir and Tinputz (all in the northern region of the province), Paruparu and Wakunai (central region), and Siwai and Buin (southern region). These initial eight district teams were the most active in SCP overall and remained active until the end of the project.

Leitana Nehan faced two political hurdles in extending its work from Buka throughout the main island of Bougainville. First its name means Buka (and) Nissan, and it was therefore not immediately associated with Bougainville island itself. Second, there were perceptions among some people on mainland Bougainville that people on Buka had sided with the PNGDF during the crisis, and this created a degree of suspicion. However, a number of historical events and cultural traditions contributed to the acceptance of Leitana Nehan in the central and southern districts of Bougainville. These included a strong relationship and commitment to reciprocation of goodwill that exists among the chiefs across Bougainville. For example, the chiefs of Siwai came to Buka for refuge during difficult times in the early 1990s and were accommodated by Helen and Kris Hakena. This act of goodwill and friendship helped Leitana Nehan when they were establishing SCP in the south. In another example, Leitana Nehan was instrumental in sending essential items such as stretchers and medicines to the Morotona hospital in the south during the mid 1990s blockade (see Chapter 3). In another case of assistance, Leitana Nehan provided BRA representatives with clothing so that they could dress appropriately to attend peace talks in 1996 (see Chapter 3). In relation to establishing the Paruparu team, it was necessary for Helen Hakena, as executive director, George Lesi, the assistant executive director, and Hilary Laris, one of the project officers (now a member of the Autonomous Bougainville Government), to conduct an intensive awareness workshop for the chiefs from villages in the mountainous areas of the northeast and areas surrounding Paruparu before they could be convinced to support the SCP project. Once this intervention had been carried out, the Chiefs from these areas proceeded eagerly to select their own team members and requested Leitana Nehan to train them, which they did.

Personal and family links were also instrumental in facilitating the work of Leitana Nehan in the central, southern and western districts. For example, the executive director's uncle was married to a woman from Wakunai and another relative had married a woman from the northwest. These links through marriage led to extended family relationships that facilitated exchanges and visits, which in turn enabled Leitana Nehan to get a stronger foothold in these distant districts for their peace-building work. In another situation, a teacher from Koromira/Koianu who had worked with Helen Hakena for several years helped Leitana Nehan to introduce programs into the area. In southeast Bougainville, community leaders in Manatai/Torau had heard how good the Leitana Nehan programs were from the Paruparu experience and hence invited Leitana Nehan to field a team in their area as well. These examples demonstrate how personal and familial relationships between people in Buka and people in other districts helped Leitana Nehan successfully overcome the challenges it faced in extending the SCP project across the mainland.

Furthermore, one of the Leitana Nehan team leaders in the central district, John Ibouko (Joseph Kabui's first cousin), who had been a commander for the BRA in the same area, used his influence to promote Leitana Nehan's work. John had been shot in the face while with the BRA in the mountains in the early 1990s. His comrades carried him down to the coast, from where he took a boat to Taro Island in the Western Province of Solomon Islands. From there he was moved to the hospital in the Solomons capital, Honiara, where he spent five years and underwent several operations to reconstruct his face. After the war, he joined Leitana Nehan and became one of its most powerful advocates in his district. He was so keen on Leitana Nehan's model of community development that he was instrumental in starting Darenai school in his district and became the first chair of the school's board of management.

ADVANCING THE PROJECT

During their first year in the field, the Leitana Nehan teams concentrated their efforts on homebrew awareness, combating violence against women and promoting women's rights, while IHD and counselling were the main focus in the second year (LNWDA 2002a). Each team aimed to visit ten communities, including a number of schools. By September 2000, the teams had conducted initial workshops in eleven schools and eleven communities (LNWDA 2000c). Through these awareness workshops, they came into contact with over 4,500 people, of which over 2,100 were women. Heavy rain was reported to have prevented the teams in Wakunai, Bana, Siwai and Buin from carrying out their awareness workshops by this stage (LNWDA 2000c), and crocodiles (see Box 4.2), armed men, transport difficulties and distance (see Boxes 4.3 and 4.4) also hindered their efforts.

As noted above, Rose Trongat, a specialist IHD trainer, was recruited as a project officer for the SCP. In the second year of the project she ran six IHD training sessions for community representatives in the three regions (south, central and north), including three follow up workshops in Buka. Community representatives and volunteers in or near Buka could access the services of the Marist Brothers and Family Life, both of which were associated with the Catholic Church and were able to provide IHD training. Although Leitana Nehan planned to hold regular IHD workshops for the community representatives, this was not feasible given the high cost of bringing representatives from over 120 communities to Buka, and it proved more viable to appoint a roving project officer to deliver IHD training in the districts. Nevertheless, 27 volunteers were brought to Buka for IHD training in the last quarter of 2000 (LNWDA, n.d.),[12] and a further 20 people were trained in Buka in the third quarter of 2001 (LNWDA 2002b). By the end of Phase 1, one or two volunteers had been trained in IHD on each team. The volunteers, and particularly the team leaders, attended regular planning and review workshops, which enabled Leitana Nehan to collect reliable data for quarterly reporting and to facilitate project implementation.

Leitana Nehan intended to find funds to send several people to Fiji for four weeks of intensive counselling training at the Women's Crisis Centre in Suva. By the end of the first year of Phase 1, Buin, Paruparu and Siwai were recognised as districts that needed counsellors (LNWDA 2001a). The overall plan was to deploy counsellors with at least basic training to a number of districts, preferably to the very areas from which they had originally come. These field counsellors could then work as mobile counsellors alongside the Leitana Nehan teams. Volunteers were selected for this purpose from areas where counselling needs were highest and also from areas that were distant and difficult to reach from the centre in Buka. This training eventually took place in May 2001 when seven counsellors were trained over four weeks in Fiji. Leitana Nehan was now in a position to deploy field counsellors to Nissan, Northwest, Tinputz, Paruparu, Buin, Siwai and Bana districts (LNWDA 2002a). Of the seven counsellors trained in Fiji, Anne Rangai, from Siwai, was also the project officer responsible for the southern Leitana Nehan teams.

By the end of March 2002 the 10 Leitana Nehan teams and 70 volunteers involved in implementing SCP Phase 1 had completed all the initial workshops for 150 communities and follow-up workshops for 60 communities and 25 schools (LNWDA 2002b). By this stage, Leitana Nehan had reached 4,934 people, of which 2,762 were women. In a letter to IWDA, Helen Hakena acknowledged the general difficulties faced by project workers during SCP phase 1. She wrote,

> [t]he organisation acknowledges the worthy contributions by volunteers, project officers, and experienced trainers. These people have walked hundreds of kilometres on foot, climbed rugged terrains, crossed flooded rivers and braved all sorts of weather, while carrying out Leitana Nehan's complex range of programs. Working in a hostile environment can be risky. The lack of a stable infrastructure like transport, communication, food supply, economical and political issues have all impacted on the SCP Project (LNWDA 2002b:n.p.).

A story in the same document indicates how delicate some of the problems were at a local level for action-oriented peace-builders. In answer to the question 'What did local people tell about their personal situations?' the following response was received.

> Three ex-combatants' wives were shot with arms after the consumption of homebrew. Threats have been issued to families when trying to resolve the matter. Communities cannot do much, especially when arms are involved in settling disputes. This alone causes a lot of fear, mistrust, insecurity and foremost instability. Almost in every community visited, Chiefs, women, men and children in schools have all discussed this fear. Fear of retaliation…when ex-combatants die by violent means, causes paralysis to the communities (LNWDA 2002b:n.p.).

Box 4.2   Waking up to a shock *Valentine Tur*

Although I usually worked on Buka, one time in 2000 I went with Ezekial Lames and Justinian Suraka to do an awareness workshop in Kunua, on the mainland of Bougainville. We walked there from Hahon, about eight hours. Much of the way was through swampy land. We walked until well after dark. It's an isolated area, with families scattered and not grouped in big villages. So when we were tired of walking, there was no village nearby in which to sleep. We decided to cross one more wide, deep river and then sleep on the sand bank on the other side. The river was deeper than we thought so we had to hold hands to keep each other from floating away. When we got to the other side, we fell asleep on the sand. In the morning we woke up. We were really sore from our long walk the previous day. We looked around and got a shock to see some big saltwater crocodiles sleeping on the opposite bank. Then we spotted some swimming in the river that we had crossed the night before. We were really frightened. It was the first time I had seen this kind of crocodile. I said to the other guys, 'Let's get out of here'. So we walked away as fast as we could, and after about an hour or two we reached Kunua government station, where we held the workshop.

The volunteers also faced physical dangers apart from those provided by wild animals and flooded rivers, as Ezekial Lames recounts (see Box 4.4).

Towards the end of phase 1 of the SCP, Leitana Nehan staff noted some of the issues that lead to an escalation of violence during the holiday season, which extends over a period of three months from November to January (LNWDA 2002c). The escalation of violence and social problems in this period was attributed to celebrations during the holiday season when many people, including public servants and school children, returning home for the Christmas holidays from other provinces of Papua New Guinea or districts within Bougainville. The teams worked during their consultations with 35 communities and 10 schools to curb the particular types of social problems that usually occur in this period. They tried to dissuade women from drinking because fights often resulted when husbands and wives both drank too much. It was noted that women also drink a lot during the festive season, which causes fights due to petty jealousies. Sexual harassment also occurred frequently when drunk men harassed women openly in public places, at dances, and even in front of relatives or family members, and this is culturally unacceptable. These incidents often resulted in fights that created disturbances in communities and among families. In addition, many families indicated that fights between fathers and sons were prevalent during this period due to a high consumption of homebrew alcohol. This scenario occurred when sons were drinking together with fathers or fathers were protecting daughters and mothers from drunken sons who would abuse them verbally or harass them physically to obtain food or money. The teams advocated strategies, such as the banning of dances and the burning of apparatus used to brew alcohol in order to minimise alcohol consumption and brewing. They hoped that these measures would contribute to minimising violence and social problems during the holiday season. In spite of these precautions, drunken men shot their wives during this period in incidents that took place in three different villages, and one woman was paralysed as a result. It is noteworthy, however, that none of these villages was actually involved in SCP.

Box 4.3   An unexpected swim *Ezekial Lames*

One time in 2001 they sent us for monitoring in Daranai, in Paruparu, near the Panguna area. We got a car in Kokopau, and it was raining heavily. It rained all day. We travelled all the way without stopping in Arawa, and then went up into the no-go zone, until about five to seven in the evening we arrived in Panguna. I was dropped by the roadside and walked for about an hour to reach a village. I didn't have a torch, and it was still raining and very dark. Up there it is like a desert, because of the copper waste that flowed down. The ground is like sand. There used to be an old crane that has been dumped there. About five minutes after the crane you turn off and you can follow an old drain down the side of the cliff to a point where you can cross the river. At that time there had been a lot of rain and the river was in flood. However, I didn't realise that the river was flooded, and when I reached the end of the drain I stepped onto the sand, but it was very slippery and I slid into the river. The water carried me away. I lost my bag, which contained my sports gear and books. The current was very strong and the water was very cold as it was coming down from high in the mountains. I tried to find something to hold on to, but it was flowing very quickly. Fortunately at a bend in the river some *pitpit* grass was hanging over and I managed to grab it and pull myself up onto the back.

I walked back to where I had fallen in, but now I was on the opposite bank. So I had to walk further up the bank until I reached a village, Tumpu, that we had passed through before crossing the river. There I called out and some people heard me. They came out and I told them what had happened. I slept in that village and the next morning I walked to Daranai primary school to do the monitoring. After that, I had to walk up to the SDA station at Konuku. After visiting this village, I walked down for two hours and stayed overnight with another family.

The next morning I left them and walked up and down another three mountains before arriving at Paruparu station at about 1pm. At Paruparu I visited the chiefs, teachers, students and religious leaders, and asked them how they felt about the awareness program that had been carried out, and the changes that they had noticed in the community, especially regarding homebrew consumption. There was also counselling occurring there, and I also asked them what else they wanted included in the program. Many of them felt it was a good program, especially about VAW and homebrew consumption.

These villages that the Paruparu team were working in are very remote villages, so it was hard for people to have access to stores. They would only go to Arawa about once a month. Thus they usually did not have access to soft drinks to mix with the homebrew, and as a result they were making very pure and strong homebrew. Domestic violence, rape and child sexual abuse were common in those areas during and after the crisis, and people had come to think that was just the way life was.

After the awareness they began to set up laws within the community, about how to deal with such things. For example, if a man hits a woman or child sexual abuse occurs, then the chiefs can adjudicate and impose fines of kina, pigs or shell money, and then people can reconcile. We talked about justice and peace through our IHD program. There must be justice and then peace. So if justice is not done, then there will be no peace. If we come and talk and say that we are reconciled, without justice, then there still will not be peace. They also set up some rules on homebrew. If they found anyone making homebrew, then they incurred a fine of both K100 and a pig, which were given to the victim, and they used the pig for a reconciliation feast. As a result, there were major changes in the community. Another result of the program in that place was that they sent twelve people down for counsellor training at Bougainville Trauma Institute. There were many people traumatised there, because the area was greatly affected by the crisis.

In response to a question about the strategies communities involved in SCP were using to reduce alcohol related violence, the report provides examples of the following deterrents.

> The schools have enforced school rules such as consumers and brewers in schools would be suspended/terminated. Community leaders have imposed fines e.g. K50 for brewing and K20 for drinking and disorderly behaviour in the village. Five men have paid fines to village magistrates (in one district) for drinking and being disorderly. Examples: bad language used and verbal harassing of women (LNWDA 2002c:n.p.).

In relation to why teams could not visit certain communities even when scheduled visits were planned, the following examples from the report provide explanations and describe the complex realities of working in a post-conflict environment where violence is simmering below the surface and events occur without warning.

> Killing in a village at Tinputz prevented a workshop already scheduled to be conducted. In Bana someone died in the community, which resulted in the team not going there at all, as the ten days of mourning had to be observed. Flooding and the rainy season also prevented the teams from carrying out their awareness workshops as scheduled (LNWDA 2002c:n.p.).

By the time Leitana Nehan had reached the end of Phase 1 of SCP, the Leitana Nehan teams had altogether followed up the initial workshops in 95 communities and 35 schools. It is somewhat unclear, however, how many of these communities had also developed and carried out strategies to actively reduce violence against women and children locally.[13] Leitana Nehan staff believed that the SCP had achieved its aims and objectives by covering most of the communities under the Project Workplan and that the field teams had carried out all the activities specified under the SCP Workplan as scheduled (LNWDA 2002c).

According to Crook (cited in Cox 2004:11), at the end of Phase 1, Leitana Nehan did not appear to have the organisational capacity to collect and process hard data to satisfy the monitoring and evaluation aims of its mentor NGO. This view reflects the values, attitudes and accountability emphasis of the donor agency, echoed by the mentor organisation, rather than being a real problem with SCP and Leitana Nehan itself. The following chapter, in which I describe the work

---

Box 4.4   A hasty departure from Kuraio *Ezekial Lames*

I was sent down to Atsinima on the border between Northwest and Torokina with Alex Bunn and Steven Kuta. We caught a boat in Buka. It had a 60hp motor, and we travelled for about three hours. We dropped some passengers at Kuraio, and then continued to Atsinima. When we got there, we went up the river for a few minutes, then they dropped us on the bank. We walked for a couple of minutes to get to the school, where we were met by the headmaster, who was a man from Nissan. We stayed overnight and slept in the staffroom. There were many mosquitoes there. I hardly slept at all. It must have been their breeding place. So we fought the mosquitoes for ages. Then the headmaster heard us killing mosquitoes, and came and brought us some coils. The place had a low ceiling, so the coils worked well and eventually we went to sleep until morning.

The headmaster asked his son to take us to the river. It was an amazingly clear river and very cold. You could throw chains and coins into the river and they were clearly visible on the river bed. The river stones were very white, like lime. I'd never seen such clean water. So we had a bath there, and went back up to the school for breakfast. This was the first awareness that had been run in that area. We only started at 10am, because we had to wait for people to come from far away in the centre of Bougainville Island. Those people came down with sugar cane, pineapple, muli (oranges), peanuts and all sorts of things. We ran the awareness and afterwards they gave us a meal. We were very happy and thanked them, while they thanked us for the program and the new ideas they had heard. But homebrew was really bad there. There had been many cases of rape and domestic violence in the previous months, including a woman who had been beaten to death. Just a few days before we arrived, there had been an incest case committed by a prominent person in the village. When we talked about those issues, people realised these kinds of actions were not good.

We left Atsinima and walked for about three hours along the coast, to visit another small village called Pukuito. There we met the paramount chief. The village comprises just one family. There are two temporary houses for fishing near the beach, and the permanent houses are up on the hill. They wanted the awareness to be carried out in the evening. They gave us a wild pig to eat. The chief greeted us with a bunch of peanuts, because when we arrived the chief's wife was bundling up peanuts. His brother-in-law, who is the chief's deputy and also the catechist in the village, came and greeted us with big bundles of tobacco. There were no stores there, so we couldn't find any manufactured tobacco products. Since I'm a smoker, I was quite happy. Then I needed to ask them for a page from the *Post-Courier* so I could make a cigarette, and they gave me one full *Post-Courier*, an old one.

The chief showed us around the village. First he showed us the cemetery. It was very clean, with nice flowers and a big cross. The chapel was made of bush materials and beautifully set up. We went down to the river, and he showed us upstream the place to fetch water, then further down, the place for men to wash, then the place for laundry and furthest downstream where all the rubbish ends up is the place for women to wash. Then they showed us the canoes that they use to travel up the coast.

We had a meal, before they rang the bell for chapel. Everybody came. I suggested that we conduct the awareness outside the chapel, in an open space, because we could light lots of fires for light. The chapel, even with candles, would be too dark. So we all came outside and they lit fires, and we conducted the awareness program. Afterwards we said lets drink tea and coffee, and when the chief heard there was coffee he was very happy, because he really liked it, and because there was none in the village. The wife brought us a big pot of boiled peanuts to eat, and they brought plenty of bananas that they cooked in the fires, and we talked and chewed betel nut and smoked and at about 3am we all went to sleep. Just before we went to sleep, a boy cried out and it sounded like a dog. He hadn't been to school during the crisis. I nicknamed him 'Guran' which is the name of the messenger in the Phantom comics, because he was short with a big belly like an African child.

When we woke up everyone came and talked to us about the awareness, which they found really useful. They prepared three canoes, which we got in at the river bank and we paddled down to the beach. It took about half an hour to reach the sea. I was in one canoe, Steven and Alex in another, and our bags and the food they gave us were in the third. We paddled up the coast for three hours. There's no road there because the land is too steep; the mountains fall directly into the sea. We took the canoes as far as Korepovi, and then we had to walk. We met a man called Fabian, and he wanted to walk to Kuraio, where we had previously dropped passengers. We told him we were going to the same place. So he offered to help us carry our bags. We walked for more than an hour along the beach. We had to cross many rivers on the way.

We arrived in Kuraio at about 4pm. We were met by the station manager, a man named Matthew. He gave us some accommodation in a room in the priest's house. In the evening he took us to the river to wash. When we came back, two couples called out to us. They gave us some cooked taro. They also had a small canteen, and I bought some tinned fish, biscuits, sugar and three packets of rice. Unknown to us, a BRA commander, drunk and armed with a gun, had arrived in Kuraio while we were washing at the river. There was another boy at the station, who had seen us walk up the river, that heard the BRA commander asking where we were. This young boy ran up and warned us. We got back to the house without the BRA commander seeing us, but when we went to go out, the BRA commander was there. I went out first. He asked who was the leader of the team. I said that I was. He put the gun to my face, and held it there for a few minutes. But then he put the gun down. He said, 'I am going away for five minutes. When I come back if I find you here, I will shoot you.'

The station manager wanted us to stay and said he would protect us. But we said we would leave, in line with Leitana Nehan's security policy. We packed our things. We found a person from Nagovisi, married to a woman from Kuraio, who had a boat, but he only had a small amount of petrol. Someone else had some petrol that he was planning to use for carrying some timber, so I offered to pay for it, since our lives were at risk. Immediately he said that was fine, but petrol was very expensive. I said that it didn't matter about the cost, because our lives were at stake. So I gave him some money and he filled up the tank. He fetched his three-year-old son, because the mother was in the garden, and we quickly pulled the boat down to the beach, hoping the BRA commander would not show up again. We made it safely to Amun and stayed overnight there. In the morning we did another awareness workshop in that village. We left Amun and walked three hours to Sipai, the Catholic Mission. We ran another awareness at the primary school there, along with the communities. We walked for about one and a half hours into a place in the bush, Mapisi Station, the district headquarters for Northwest. We slept at the primary school. We conducted three awareness workshops in Mapisi: one at the school and two in the communities, over two days. Then we walked another 30 minutes to a place called Number 10 Village. We got a boat there and followed the river down to the coast, and then back to Buka.

A few months later we did a follow-up workshop in many of the same villages. This time there were six of us, including the project officer, Benedicta Noneng. We took the boat to Atsinima, and then walked to Korepovi, Pukuito and Kuraio, where we only stayed a few minutes to buy biscuits and for one team member to go into the bush and take off their underwear, which was causing a rash; we never wore underwear out there because they chaffed from getting wet in the rivers and from sweat. Then we walked to Amun and Sipai, then over the mountains to Mapisi, and on to Number 10 village. We crossed a few more rivers, including one in which the water was over our heads and we had to hold our breath and carry our bags on our outstretched arms, and we rescued Quentin when he sank into the mud up to his neck, before we finally reached another village on the coast. When we told them we had walked from Atsinima, they couldn't believe it, and said that they'd never heard of anyone walking that far before. They also mentioned that no one ever crossed the last river before the village, where a young girl was taken by a crocodile only a month earlier.

carried out by Leitana Nehan in July 2003, shows that monthly reporting was relatively advanced by the middle of Phase 2 of SCP but the information was not as rich in stories and lessons from the field as it was in the Phase 1 reporting, because the mentor NGO's reporting requirements and format had changed. In many ways the stories told in Phase 1 were more useful indicators of what was actually taking place.

With an additional seven trained counsellors working with teams by the end of Phase 1, counselling services were brought closer to women in the communities, and the number of clients apparently increased in this last quarter (LNWDA 2002c). The reasons for the increase, apart from the deployment of field counsellors, included the fact that women were more willing to talk freely to counsellors who spoke their language and were from their own people. For instance, rape victims from as far back as the period 1990–97 were now coming forward for counselling (LNWDA 2002c). The deployment of field counsellors resulted in an increase in awareness about issues such as rape and domestic violence and subsequently this became evident in the counselling statistics (LNWDA 2002c). Having mobile counsellors within districts enabled Leitana Nehan to cut transport costs substantially.

CONCLUSION

Helen made following comments at the end of the SCP.

> We have learned that public relations and networking with communities, authorities and NGOs on the ground has helped the SCP project to be supported well by

communities. Through the years we were able to identify and study our target groups in different areas to gain our points of entry into the communities. Our influence, approaches and flexibility among different groups of people have gained us the support and respect of everyone in the communities under the SCP workplans. Our strength lies in the support network of volunteers who work in the 150 communities across Bougainville. The skills of staff and trainers have also contributed to the effective running of the organisation and also to project management. In the last two years of Phase 1 we feel that we have achieved our aims and objectives by promoting and contributing to the restoration of peace on Bougainville and promotion of a non-violent society (LNWDA 2002c:n.p.)

The main success of the SCP project in Phase 1 could be attributed to the design and organisation of the project and in its implementation processes, which were supported by continuous training. Specifically, the three-pronged approach employed by Leitana Nehan involved project management and counselling support from a central office in Buka; a radio program, written media coverage and the creative activities of the theatre troupe reinforcing local capacity-building; and field teams working tirelessly to engage with local community representatives and liaise with community leaders. The combined effects of these SCP support programs contributed to conflict transformation in local communities. In this sense, SCP Phase 1 was a success. SCP Phase 2 built on the foundations provided by SCP Phase 1. The details of activities conducted by Leitana Nehan in SCP Phase 2 are discussed in the next chapter.

Counselling became a major focus for the teams by the end of SCP Phase 1. In short, the counselling needs in communities were greater than the project was designed to accommodate. The high demand for counselling, in combination with the problems associated with delivering a counselling service from the central office in Buka, as I have already discussed, prompted Leitana Nehan to seek funds to improve the counselling skills of selected team members. These were issues that Leitana Nehan had to contend with as they were planning for Phase 2.

NOTES

[1]   The IHD program and its approach to development are discussed in Chapter 6. It is a system used by the Roman Catholic Church to reduce social problems in the

community. IHD is described in the Leitana Nehan proposal (LNWDA and IWDA 1999:10) as 'a holistic approach to community development that highlights the interrelatedness of social problems'.

2   The second SCP objective was 'to strengthen Leitana Nehan's ability to effectively manage and implement its program and to plan future activities by ensuring appropriate staffing and training in organisational, program and office management'.

3   The details of the partnership aspect of NGO activities and the relationships that developed between Leitana Nehan, IWDA and AusAID are discussed in Chapter 7.

4   Leitana Nehan was nominated for the Millennium Peace Prize, which it subsequently won in recognition of its peace-building work with women in Bougainville.

5   Executive Director Helen Hakena and Assistant Executive Director George Lesi both reported that the radio programs enhanced the work of the field teams. The radio program was broadcast through Radio Bougainville every Thursday at 6pm, and there were 40 or more broadcasts per annum.

6   A number of Leitana Nehan staff and volunteer trainers underwent training in trauma counselling through the 'Family Life Team' run by the Catholic Church. Matters relating to marriage counselling were often referred to 'Family Life'. In addition, people needing legal advice were referred to the public prosecutor and private lawyers. Seven people were sent to Fiji in May 2001 for counselling training (Leitana Nehan n.d.).

7   The New Zealand High Commission funded the International Women's Day Celebrations.

8   The topics covered in this workshop for youth in Buka included: organisational structure; functions, roles and responsibilities of an organisation; characteristics of a leader; writing and working with job descriptions; communication skills, compilation of a community profile; effective networking; working well with people; setting objectives and planning activities; basic project management; and the preparation of workplans (LNWDA 2001a:8).

9   LNWDA carries out advocacy work with respect to women's rights on behalf of the silent majority of women in Bougainville. It speaks out about issues such as the fair representation of women in politics, administration and decision-making, as well as advocating to stop violence against women (LNWDA 2001a:10).

10   The topics covered in the police training included: gender sensitivity, religion, culture, socioeconomic issues and violence against women, violence as a human rights issue, domestic violence, rape, sexual harassment, the convention on rights of the child, counselling skills, legal literacy, lobbying and advocacy, all of which are relevant to objectives in SCP.

[11] BOCBHIP was concentrating mainly on health related problems that were affecting people living in and around the care centres during the Bougainville conflict.

[12] The Notable Events document covered the organisation's activities between 1992–2003. This information was reported for the year 2000.

[13] There is a gap in reporting for 2002, a period during which all the obligations, targets and reporting for SCP Phase 1 had to be finalised to the satisfaction of the donor and mentor before SCP Phase 2 could be funded. This is common practice, in which later stages of a project are contingent on fulfilment of reporting requirements for completion of earlier stages. Unfortunately, this can too often lead to the loss of experienced staff and trainers who are forced to take up other paid work during the funding-flow interruption.

5　FROM PEACE TO PROGRESS

Bert Jenkins

Following the completion of Phase 1 of the Strengthening Communities for Peace (SCP) project, Leitana Nehan obtained funding for a second phase of the project with the same name but subtitled 'From Peace to Progress'. Phase 2 ran over a period of 13 months between January 2003 and February 2004. Like Phase 1, Phase 2 emphasised personal development, particularly Integral Human Development (IHD), but also stressed community development through the strengthening of civil society and good governance at both the community and state levels (Cox 2004b). This emphasis had potentially important consequences for Bougainville, which was preparing at the time to become an autonomous region of Papua New Guinea under a new constitution. The main challenge in Phase 2 was not merely meeting set targets in SCP but also working in a gender sensitive way at all levels of activities that Leitana Nehan conducted. As with Phase 1, Phase 2 ran in parallel to other activities that supported the overarching project objective of 'advancing the role of women in society'.

ASSOCIATED ACTIVITIES THAT SUPPORTED SCP OBJECTIVES

During the period 2003–04, Leitana Nehan staff and volunteers were involved in a range of activities that directly or indirectly contributed to the goals of SCP Phase 2. Leitana Nehan met with various organisations in Bougainville to promote arms disposal in March 2003 (LNWDA 2003b). The Bougainville Alliance of

Community Development Agencies and the Buka District Council of Women also were present at these deliberations. These meetings and advocacy activities were possible because the executive director, Helen Hakena, was closely associated with the Buka District Council of Women and was a' prominent chief with authority to discuss women's issues and the peace process with respect to her matrilineal connections in North Bougainville.[1] This authority made it possible for her to facilitate these meetings herself. A commitment to the ceasefire, the disposal of arms and a culture of peace were all essential preconditions for the peace-building work that Leitana Nehan was carrying out in Bougainville through SCP.

In March 2003, Helen toured Australia with the IWDA, talking to various women's groups about Leitana Nehan's work. This was part of Leitana Nehan's obligations as a recipient of the Millennium Peace Prize. In July 2003, Helen spoke at a Peace Symposium at the University of New England in Armidale about women's suffering in Bougainville (LNWDA 2003b). In September 2003, Helen was invited to Port Moresby to address a conference on 'women's rights', where she spoke about violence against women in the context of the plight of women during armed conflicts and in post-conflict situations (LNWDA 2003b). These opportunities allowed Helen, as Executive Director of Leitana Nehan, to promote and publicise the organisations work in Bougainville to an international audience.

In October 2003, Helen provided training for a World Vision project on 'Water Sanitation', a serious community development and public health issue, where she focused on issues of 'gender and development' (Hakena 2004).

Apart from being the executive director of Leitana Nehan, Helen held other important positions of responsibility. By the end of 2004, Helen Hakena was the secretary of the PNG Community Development Scheme (CDS), a member of the Provincial Education Board, and chair of the Provincial Literacy Programme.

In March 2003, George Lesi, the assistant executive director, was invited to provide input to a joint Provincial Government meeting on the 'recognition of women in the draft constitution' (LNWDA 2003b:n.p.). George was also invited to address important meetings that involved the community, civil society agencies, private companies and the government. In July 2003, he represented Leitana Nehan in speaking engagements at the PNG Islands Development Forum and the NGO Mining Conference (LNWDA 2003b). Another valuable service that George undertook was to assist in data collection for a Small Arms Survey project on gun-running in Papua New Guinea, which showed how weapons left Bougainville after the conflict and ended up in the Southern Highlands of Papua New Guinea (Alpers 2005). Leitana Nehan also sent him to attend professional development courses overseas, including a human rights training workshop in Thailand in 2003.[2] Human rights issues, particularly for women and children, were an important focus of the SCP project.

Another Leitana Nehan workshop that had a major impact on women's lives was a seven-day training course for fifteen village birth attendants on the remote atoll of Nissan held in November 2003 (see box below). The course was coordinated by Agnes Titus and delivered by Cathleen Loadsman.

SCP PHASE 2 PROJECT DESIGN AND ORGANISATION

Whereas there were 10 team leaders and 40 volunteer assistants in SCP Phase 1, Phase 2 saw these numbers increase to 13 team leaders and 78 volunteers, a total of 91 individuals. The 13 teams were located in Nissan, Buka, Selau/Suir, Tinputz, Wakunai, Paruparu, Buin, Siwai, Bana, Northwest, Manatai/Torau, Koromira/Koianu and Torokina. The three new teams were located at Torokina in the west, and Koramira/Koianu and Manetai/Torau in the coastal districts of the central-southeast part of Bougainville Island. Although the new teams had commenced relatively late and only as Phase 1 neared completion, they were still active at the end of Phase 2. Nine teams were active on mainland Bougainville at the beginning of Phase 2; two additional teams—Bana from the southwest and a generic team from the Northwest—became active in the later stages of Phase 2.[3] Although these teams had been identified early on in SCP, they were relatively slow to develop, and this late start meant that training activities planned for team leaders, volunteers and community representatives had to be repeated and fast-tracked. Experienced staff

Box 5.1   Saving mothers' and babies' lives on Nissan Atoll
Agnes Titus

I got on the small Airlink plane at Nissan airport to go to Buka for a Leitana Nehan review in early 2003. On the flight, which had originated in Rabaul, was Cathleen Loadsman, a trained nurse, who was working in Arawa, and was involved in the village birth attendants' training on mainland Bougainville and in other parts of Papua New Guinea. We got talking about the state of affairs of women in Nissan and I recounted a recent incident of a mother giving birth in a canoe. I told Cathleen that I had been the President of the Tungol Catholic Women's Association since 1992, and that safe motherhood had always been an issue. There had been numerous instances where mothers gave birth in the villages, only trying to get to a health facility in emergencies. Many women had given birth in trucks, boats or under trees on their way to a health facility.

Nissan has one health centre and six aid posts. Because of the difficulties families face, such as a general lack of money, especially for transport and health facility fees, I made the request to Cathleen to try and find some funds to train the Nissan traditional birth attendants. She found some money, and the training was undertaken from 1–7 November 2003. At the closing ceremony, the women from the villages came together at Tungol and put on dances and sang in thanksgiving to the facilitators and coordinator for bringing home to them one answer to their issues, and saving their lives.

The three facilitators stayed at my home, and every morning, my husband Michael took us by boat across to Tungol Catholic Mission where the training was being held, and picked us up in the afternoon. The participants were accommodated at the mission. While on Nissan, Cathleen saw a young girl named Rose who was a victim of violence, unmarried and pregnant. Cathleen found that she had an enlarged spleen, and advised her to go to the health centre when she was ready. Just seven days after the workshop had finished, and after Cathleen had gone back home to her job at Prince Albert Hospital in Sydney, Cathy Rangai, who had just done the training, was called, along with the health worker at Mapiri aid post, Romanus. I also went along to help out if needed. To our amazement, Rose delivered normally a beautiful girl, which was named after Cathleen Loadsman.

Was it worthwhile? Yes! The VBA course had many important outcomes

- Rose Mako and Magorina Tondiat went full swing immediately after the workshop to raise awareness of the people of Yotchibol village about their role as VBAs.
- Daling Ute attended to six pregnancies in Kulis village.
- Cathrine Miriki has attended to all the pregnancies in Tanaheran village. All were successful, including her own daughter's (Takaku). Takaku's pregnancy was quite a difficult one, and she had to go to the Tungol aid post. She was later referred to the Kalil Health Centre and Cathrine told me that she delivered her grandson herself. There was no nurse in attendance.
- Rose Kaes and Alberta Nemon accompanied their pregnant friends to Buka District Hospital when they developed complications, having been referred from the Kalil Health Centre in Nissan.
- Nerry Libika, who was a member of the SCP team on Nissan, arrived at an awareness workshop in New Camp very sleepy one day after being up all night helping a young girl give birth. She was a single girl, unsure, and very poor as well. She gave birth with Nerry's assistance by the light from a small bottle lamp, as no one had a torch.
- Many men have come to support the VBAs more. For example, Lisa Nicky's husband, Luis, is one of the proudest and best supporters of the VBAs. This is because he has witnessed the challenges Lisa encounters when delivering babies at their village in Balil. 'She is helping a lot of women, including difficult births', says Luis.

This is a beautiful story for me and the women of Nissan, because we are isolated and impoverished. But we have proven that skills training can make a difference in our lives: the village birth attendants are saving lives on Nissan.

had to redouble their efforts to support and help the new teams catch up in terms of planning, project activities and training.

Each team had a team leader and six volunteers. At the start of Phase 2, one of these volunteers was either a counsellor with some basic training or assisted in collecting counselling information (LNWDA 2003b). Subsequently, however, all teams had trained counsellors and in some cases an additional trained assistant. Many of these counsellors were trained in basic counselling skills during Phase 2, when the bulk of the grassroots counselling and intensive interaction with community groups took place.[4]

Every team had the task of developing two 'community case studies' and were expected to visit these communities four times before the end of Phase 2 (LNWDA 2003b). This meant that they had to concentrate their efforts in a few communities. However, the teams were required to also visit three other communities at least twice, including among them a number of selected schools (LNWDA 2003b). Therefore Phase 2, unlike Phase 1, was more intensive in that each team had to spend more time in two out of five selected communities. Activities in communities that were visited only twice were similar to those carried out in Phase 1: an initial visit to raise awareness and a follow up visit to organise progress towards the development of local strategies. In Phase 2, the teams were trained to monitor progress in their case study communities in order to tailor appropriate violence-prevention strategies that specifically suited the prevailing conditions in a particular location (LNWDA 2003b). This flexibility in Phase 2 gave team leaders the opportunity to make independent decisions with regard to implementing changes on the ground, depending on their own assessment of a situation. It made sense to allow experienced team leaders to instigate informed decisions, and the flexibility also indicates that a degree of trust had been established in team leaders' capabilities. Team leaders were encouraged in Phase 2 to monitor field activities and document 'lessons learned' from case studies and community consultations. They could share these lessons with other teams during workshops and apply them in their deliberations with community groups during subsequent visits.

The first few months of Phase 2 were spent training the teams in organisational capacity-building skills, community development, governance issues, monitoring and project planning. This training took place through the strategic planning and 'training of trainers' workshops (LNWDA 2003b). The teams spent the initial three months of Phase 2 locating suitable communities and schools for workshops and case studies. The teams that started late had some catching up to do before they commenced project work with their respective communities.

ADVANCING THE PROJECT

By the middle of 2003 the teams were noticing that a number of women who had learned about their rights were now seeking additional assistance, forming groups to support each other, and participating more in community workshops than they had in Phase 1 (LNWDA 2003b). Increased acceptance of women working in decision-making roles was also reported at the community level. In addition, women were accessing resources and opportunities with less difficulty. Furthermore, the teams reported a general acknowledgment in the communities of the positive role women had played in transforming society from a culture of violence towards one of peace (LNWDA 2003b).

Helen witnessed many examples of changed conflict resolution strategies resulting from the workshops in the communities. In one case, Helen, Delphine Lesi and Hazel Geto (a woman from Buka who wanted to see the work first hand) went to the village of Teabes in Tinputz district to conduct project monitoring. They had to travel by boat because there was a roadblock between Buka and Tinputz. When they arrived at the village at about 1.30pm, the team volunteers (Fabian, Ezekial and Linus) and members of the community were already assembled for the follow-up workshop. Just before the workshop there had been a fight, and Helen suggested to the people that it might not be a suitable time to run the program. The chiefs, however, wanted it to go ahead because if it did not then the fights would continue; they also wanted to gain skills to deal with the drinking and drug-related problems prevalent in the area at the time.

On the same day as the workshop, the people who had been fighting, who were from the village of Dios, returned by car. They were angry with a family in Teabes and they went into their house and vandalised the place. They broke all the plates, and smashed up the kitchen. The people wanted to retaliate, but the chiefs said, 'You've heard the awareness, there are better ways of solving this problem than fighting in return. We will have to find strategies to solve this problem'. Helen and her colleagues stayed into the evening, discussing the issue with the chiefs. The older chiefs chose some young chiefs to meet with the chiefs from Dios. As a result of this meeting, the chiefs from both areas agreed that instead of further retaliation, the young men who had done the damage would replace the utensils and rebuild the kitchen, and they did in due course.

This monitoring visit also provided an example of how certain cultural practices have impacted on the conduct of workshops in the villages. When Helen and her friends were introduced, chiefs from about 20 different villages were sitting in the front row on the ground, not on platforms. According to their custom, the visitors had to kneel on the ground to honour the chiefs. They had to remain kneeling while they introduced themselves, and when the volunteers started to talk about various issues such as women's and children's rights. When Helen was talking, the people, who were sitting on the ground behind the chiefs, had to strain their necks to see her, because she was still kneeling down. Then Helen said, 'is it okay if we stand up? There are plenty of people here who can't see us and its good if they can see our faces while we are speaking'. Then one of the paramount chiefs said, 'I'm sorry, Helen is a female chief of Buka so she has the same power as we chiefs here, so she can stand up, and don't you people say bad things about her'. In addition to being a chief, Helen's clan was well known in that area and she had relatives there. If it had been an ordinary woman who asked to stand up while the chiefs remained seated, they would have asked for a pig as compensation. Helen was able to stand up to deliver her talk, but the other volunteers could not. When they did a role-play, they had to move away from where the people were seated so that they were not looking down on the chiefs.

Another result of this incident was that Leitana Nehan met Fidelis Dana, one of the negotiators who went to the Dios. He later became a board member of Leitana Nehan. When Helen and her friends left the village that evening, they went on to conduct another awareness program in another village. It was dark, and they travelled by wooden canoe with no outrigger through a swamp, while the volunteers walked through the swamp alongside them, steadying and guiding the canoe.

As well as undertaking monitoring visits, the central office staff were organising activities to promote peace throughout the province. Leitana Nehan held a meeting of Bougainville women to gather information and discuss weapons disposal (Stage III of the peace process), views on the imminent withdrawal of the Peace Monitoring Group (PMG), and women's participation in the peace process, including constitutional reform (LNWDA 2003b). Over 200 women participated in this meeting to advance women's role in decision-making. They came from across all districts in Bougainville, including the no-go zone. Leitana Nehan also participated in two District Women's Council meetings with the Peace Monitoring Group and UN Observer Mission to discuss strategies to speed up weapons disposal, which was holding up the peace process (LNWDA 2003b). The disposal of all weapons was necessary before the election for autonomy could take place. These issues were related directly to the objectives of Phase 2 in that the removal of guns from armed groups was essential to reduce societal violence. Leitana Nehan participated in the North Bougainville Women's Leaders meeting in June 2003, with the UN Ambassador and an advisor from the New Zealand police, to discuss security leading up to the elections, weapons disposal and the training of more women for the Bougainville Transitional Police (LNWDA 2003b). In addition, Leitana Nehan met with the Bougainville Constitutional Committee (BCC) and UNICEF to lobby for the inclusion of clauses in the new constitution in support of women's and children's rights (LNWDA 2003b). Leitana Nehan, in partnership with UNICEF, also visited primary schools in the district to discuss women's and children's rights with teachers and parents. Leitana Nehan met with the families of police personnel to discuss domestic violence issues (LNWDA 2003b).

A few infrastructure improvements took place in June–July 2003. By June 2003, the Leitana Nehan office in Buka had new toilet and showering facilities for staff and visitors, which at last met basic sanitation requirements for workers (LNWDA 2003b). A new electricity generator was installed in July to provide auxiliary power because the mains supply was very unreliable (LNWDA 2003b).

By July 2003, the teams had identified the communities that would provide the case studies for the project (LNWDA 2003b). In fact, by that time 15 out of 26 case studies were reported as nearing completion (LNWDA 2003b). In the case communities, the teams' emphasis was on promoting the formation of community-based organisations in the districts, using the training that teams and volunteers had received in organisational development and project planning. The teams helped build organisational capacity among existing and new community groups, by organising community groups and community-based organisations to write project proposals and apply for funding for their own local projects (LNWDA 2003b). The Tinputz team, for example, worked with the Tiop community to develop a water tank project, which secured funding through the PNG Community Development Scheme (CDS). In Siwai, the Tomongo Youth Group (a group of ex-combatants) received funding from NZ Aid for capacity-building training in community development and gender awareness. In Buin, the Kuhala Women's Group successfully developed a proposal for CDS funding to develop a small rice mill, and the Loait village also put in four 2,000 gallon water tanks and associated fittings. Funding for another rice mill was also obtained.

It is also interesting to note that the reporting format required by IWDA differed between the two phases of the project. In Phase 2 a set tabular format was used, providing less space for real stories from the field, which had been part of the reporting format adopted in Phase 1. Stories from the field are very useful to understanding what is actually happening on the ground with respect to community peace-building. The streamlining and formalising of the reporting process therefore actually reduced the richness of information being provided to the Leitana Nehan office in Buka and to IWDA.

Leitana Nehan experienced a number of difficulties in the middle of 2003 (LNWDA 2003b). First, Radio Bougainville decided to charge the organisation a fee for using its service, a cost for which Leitana Nehan had not budgeted. In another temporary setback to the work being done by Leitana Nehan, a total blackout over a period of six weeks disrupted the radio program and other project activities being carried out through the Buka office.

A decline in law and order was evident in the middle of 2003 with police unable to uphold the law or protect women from violence (LNWDA 2003b). Leitana Nehan met with local police to address this issue and lobbied leaders and the government to rebuild the Court House so that law-breakers could be duly prosecuted before a magistrate, a move to reinstate the judicial system, which had been totally disrupted during the conflict. Leitana Nehan representatives met with a joint Law and Order Committee from New Zealand Aid and AusAID to discuss law and order issues in Bougainville. The NGO reported an escalation of violence against women and called for laws and action by the police and the judiciary to reduce problems associated with alcohol abuse in society (LNWDA 2003b). Violence against women was increasing despite the many awareness workshops run by groups such as Leitana Nehan to reduce violence in post-conflict Bougainville. These interactions with the police, the PNG government and bilateral aid agencies indicates how Leitana Nehan was willing to move outside its NGO role as project manager to deal with issues that were directly related to its core business of standing up for women's rights and the elimination of violence against women. Specifically, however, this reflects the understanding that the SCP project will be more successful if the police and the judiciary are able to carry out their proper functions in society.

During the middle months of 2003, Leitana Nehan continued its own organisational development and energetically engaged with bilateral aid, international and civil society agencies to build a more peaceful Bougainville (LNWDA 2003b). For example, Leitana Nehan was networking with international NGOs such as UNICEF, World Vision and Caritas, as well as with the Peace Monitoring Group and the United Nations Observer Mission in Bougainville (UNOMB).

Furthermore, it participated as a prominent player in meetings of the local Bougainville Alliance of Community Development Agencies (BACDA) (LNWDA 2003b).

During 2003, Leitana Nehan started working on a new strategic plan for 2004–07, with the assistance of an independent consultant based in Fiji, Colleen Taylor-Peacock (LNWDA 2003b). It also met with representatives from New Zealand Aid and AusAID to discuss future development assistance funding. The organisation was also increasingly recognised as a key agency for peace and advocacy in the region. For instance, Leitana Nehan was officially recognised for its peace work within Bougainville when it received an award at a ceremony in Arawa from the Peace Monitoring Group before it departed in July (LNWDA 2003b).

The middle of 2003 was a precarious period for peace workers in Bougainville because they were all concerned about whether armed violence would break out soon after the PMG left the country. One of their concerns was that guns disposal had not proceeded as planned in the Bougainville Peace Agreement. Although the Bougainville Resistance Forces (BRF) had surrendered their guns readily in accordance with the peace plan, it seemed that certain pockets of BRA were still reluctant to part with their weapons (LNWDA 2003b). The fear was that reluctance by certain BRA groups to disarm would prompt the resistance movement to rearm and the whole peace process would consequently be set back considerably. It was under these politically unstable circumstances that Helen was invited by the United Nations to attend the Third Biennial Conference on Small Arms. Unfortunately, communication problems between the PNG government and the Bougainville administration delayed the passage of funds and as a result the trip did not eventuate. Nevertheless, Leitana Nehan continued to campaign for weapons disposal and was subsequently invited to a negotiation meeting to discuss weapons disposal strategies (LNWDA 2003b).

An opportunity finally arose in the middle of Phase 2 to provide basic counselling training to a number of people in Bougainville, in line with Leitana Nehan's SCP aims. The Fiji Women's Crisis Centre conducted a training course on basic counselling skills for 42 participants (24 women and 18 men) in Buka in August 2003 (LNWDA 2003b). Of the 42 participants, 26 were Leitana Nehan volunteers, some of whom were attending the course to refresh the basic skills acquired through earlier training and experience in the field. The completion of this training meant that all the Leitana Nehan teams comprised trained counsellors and some teams an assistant counsellor as well. The newly acquired skills helped teams deal with the increasing demands for counselling, particularly among victims of violence and rape, in districts across Bougainville. Violence escalated sharply during the second half of 2003, with increases in rapes, fights, murders and domestic disputes reported by Leitana Nehan teams and in police caseloads (LNWDA 2003b). The teams in the field were reporting back that women were now more willing to speak out against violence, report violent incidents and stand up for their rights confidently when faced with violence, than prior to SCP (LNWDA 2003b). For example, one woman who came to an early workshop was very shy, but she went on to become a Leitana Nehan team leader. In 2004, she was walking to visit a school in her new capacity as District Women's Facilitator, working with education inspectors, when she was stopped by some men who accused her of breaking custom by speaking out publicly and taking a leadership role. However, she countered that she was not taking over their leadership role, but just giving relevant information to parents and communities about how they can rebuild the schools themselves instead of waiting for the government to provide funds. This instance reflects the increase in women's confidence, and is in large part a positive reflection on Leitana Nehan's work to empower women and prevent the escalation of violence.

In the second half of 2003, the Bougainville Transitional Team invited Leitana Nehan to work with women's groups across Bougainville to put forward a position on weapons disposal (LNWDA 2003b). This was in preparation for the joint meeting of representatives including the PNG government, the Bougainville People's Congress and the UN Observer Mission to negotiate final terms and conditions for autonomy before an election date was set. The meeting was to take place on 9 September 2003. Leitana Nehan, in its advocacy role, was lobbying for 10 women (five from the North and five from the South) to participate in these proceedings in order to ensure that women's views and broader community views on weapons disposal were represented at the highest levels.

In September 2003, Leitana Nehan organised and ran a special training course for institutional leaders in the area of conflict transformation over two five-day periods (LNWDA 2003b). A total of 73 people enrolled in this training course (45 men and 28 women). The training was well attended and over-enrolled, as the course had initially been planned to accommodate only 40 participants. Participants included nurses, police personnel, teachers, school principals and magistrates. Community feedback following the training indicated that the police had made a commitment to improving the way that they dealt with cases of violence in relation to women's rights and children's rights (rape, incest, domestic violence, sexual harassment). They were also more willing or less afraid to take cases to court. For example, the community was able to convince the police to detain two men charged with rape for a lengthy period in order to maintain community safety (LNWDA 2003b).

Box 5.2   Healing communities in the mountains of Suir
Fabian Kotsin

We started in Tekokni community. It's right up in the Suir area, in the mountains. They are a bit far from the main road. You have to climb up past Dios. We went up there and stayed there. Many people had realised that homebrew was causing a lot of fights. There was one woman from that community, who was a nurse, Mrs Tave, who was in our team, so we were able to work closely with the people there. They didn't know about rape and incest or the problems caused by homebrew.

When we did the awareness program, the chiefs were really enthusiastic about the homebrew issues. Everyone came and we were sitting there talking to them. It was the first time they had heard about women's rights. Then the women began to stand up for themselves. There's one area up there, Arabia, and one thing that happened there as a result of our homebrew awareness program was that the chiefs banned all the homebrewing. The paramount chief was Thomas. They completely banned homebrew making and consumption. All alcohol was banned at that time. If you were found drinking, they'd punish you by making you cut the grass in the school.

Leitana Nehan was also able to extend its work beyond the local level by training community leaders and government agency personnel who were in a position to address violence in society more broadly. The government and community will play a crucial role in achieving Leitana Nehan's SCP goal of reducing societal violence across Bougainville. Leitana Nehan is an excellent example of a peace-building NGO actively engaging the community, civil society and state agencies in bringing about desired social change. The organisation has led the way in demonstrating how civil society groups can work with community and government support to rebuild a society following conflict.

Towards the end of 2003, reports of firearms being produced in public around Buka surfaced, the post-conflict administrative and commercial centre of Bougainville, at a time when the entire district was meant to be completely free of weapons. Specific reports in this period suggested particular groups' use of weapons was prompting other groups to consider rearming by purchasing weapons illegally from outside Bougainville (LNWDA 2003b). In response to these problems and the general escalation of violence, Leitana Nehan rallied the support of 400 women (LNWDA 2003b) and staged a peace march.[5] The women specifically called for completion of weapons disposal in line with the UN-led peace process; reconvening of the courts in Buka to hear the hundreds of outstanding cases; implementation of existing laws on rape, incest and child abuse; a total ban on the illegal brewing of alcohol; and maintaining a state of peace in Bougainville.

All these messages were reinforced on the Leitana Nehan radio program that was broadcast across Bougainville every week. Moreover, all of the issues raised were of great importance to the success of the SCP project. The protest organised by Leitana Nehan expresses the activist role that it can play as a civil society agency in promoting non-violence and in highlighting the fact that taking up weapons again would derail the peace process and undermine the work carried out by peace-makers and peace-builders. As a women's development agency, it was capable of promoting the concerns of women in Bougainville, who have marched for peace and disarmament before and are widely recognised as important peace-makers in the community.

In the remaining months of Phase 2, between November 2003 and February 2004, Leitana Nehan concentrated its efforts on writing a proposal for a new project that would follow SCP, to be undertaken with New Zealand Aid and UNICEF (LNWDA 2003b).[6] Otherwise, the organisation spent most of its time during this period completing Phase 2 by endeavouring to meet its targets for community development, counselling, monitoring, awareness workshops and the case study visits, as well as finalising reporting requirements. Leitana Nehan ran a Community Development Training (CDT) workshop for 12 community leaders (9 men and 3 women) from across the districts. The workshop ran for five days from 3–7 November 2003. In its final workshop in Phase 2, Leitana Nehan conducted a joint awareness exercise for police personnel and health workers on 'violence against women and the law'. Women's rights and children's rights were the main issues raised during the workshop (LNWDA 2003b). These last two workshops concluded the community consultation part of Phase 2 in view of empowering women and men to work together to end the violence in Bougainville.

EVALUATION OF SCP PHASE 2

At the end of SCP Phase 2, an independent assessor evaluated the project to determine how well objectives had been met and the extent to which the expected social outcomes had been achieved. Elizabeth Cox found during the evaluation that women with a close association with Leitana Nehan were more likely than not to be vocal about issues relating to violence against women and equity for women in leadership roles (Cox 2004b). According to Cox (2004b), the SCP project had successfully addressed the violence in society through awareness workshops and interactions with local communities. The field activities carried out by the Leitana Nehan teams positively affected the personal lives of many individuals and families—over 50 per cent of those consulted at the community level felt that the project had reduced the incidence of wife beating and homebrew consumption. The project had facilitated the participation of women in general, young people in particular, in examining their social problems. In addition, a number of team leaders and community representatives reported significant reductions in both homebrew production and alcohol-related conflict among communities in which the Leitana Nehan teams had been active. Community action to surrender arms and the equipment used to brew alcohol was widespread.

A significant proportion of men and women interviewed during this evaluation process had received some kind of direct training through Leitana Nehan, and more than half these people affirmed Leitana Nehan's importance in making a real difference to their lives (Cox 2004b). According to Cox (2004b), SCP made a number of important contributions to the peace efforts. First, it contributed to building a new values system in Bougainville based on human rights and social justice. Second, community leaders (chiefs, teachers, hospital staff, magistrates, police) held the organisations' grassroots activities to promote conflict transformation in high regard. Third, SCP had facilitated 'active citizenship' among women and men in Bougainville through membership and involvement in local community-based organisations, local governance instruments (committees and boards, the constitutional reform group), community service institutions (schools, hospitals and clinics), and partnerships with other civil society organisations in peace and development movements. Fourth, SCP contributed to transformation of individual's lives by, for instance, empowering men to move away from alcohol abuse, become committed fathers and responsible husbands, and by improving people's spiritual outlook, all of which contributed to enhancing the economic well-being of families (Cox 2004b).

Although counselling was an important part of the project, Cox found it difficult to evaluate this aspect of SCP due to the sensitive nature of the work. Nevertheless, community leaders, including chiefs and teachers, counted the Leitana Nehan counsellors as allies. All communities visited during the evaluation of SCP stated that Leitana Nehan counsellors had contributed much to conflict resolution and transformation in the districts (Cox 2004b).

In general, Cox's (2004b) observations amounted to a positive evaluation of how the SCP project had contributed to human/social development and to strengthening civil society across post-conflict Bougainville. The leaders of the Leitana Nehan teams showed commitment to community education and empowerment. Community leaders were impressed by the broad experience of the Leitana Nehan team leaders, who were able to wear many different caps in playing their part in community empowerment. This diversity helped the team leaders work cooperatively with other field-based organisations such as the Peace Foundation Melanesia. They were also able to build and maintain successful community alliances through effective networking and hence were in a strong position to facilitate local activities and contribute on multiple fronts beyond their immediate duties in the SCP project (Cox 2004b).

In evaluating Leitana Nehan's role in empowering women and raising their standing in society, Cox (2004b) identified a number of cases that reveal how this had changed opportunities for women. These include the recruitment of a number of women into the new police force in Bougainville; the appointment of three women representatives to the Bougainville Consitutional Committee, the body responsible for drafting a constitution for the newly-autonomous region; the demonstration of women's leadership capacities in Leitana Nehan and the willingness of men to work under women leaders;[7] and the education and mobilisation of women to participate in a new society, speak out for their rights and protest against violence.

Leitana Nehan was recognised in 2004 as an important actor in conflict transformation when it was awarded the runner-up prize at the Fourth Pacific Human Rights Awards for outstanding work in peace and reconciliation advocacy and for the promotion of human rights for women and children in Bougainville during times of war and peace (Cox 2004b). Leitana Nehan's excellent regional and global networking had enabled it to integrate local action, global thinking, learning and solidarity, greatly improving its effectiveness, a result amply demonstrated by the successes of the SCP project (Cox 2004b). Leitana Nehan now has the capacity to build peace across Bougainville though 13 district-based teams, a trained volunteer base of over 90 committed people, and many more enthusiastic community-based representatives working alongside the teams to bring peace to their communities. Leitana Nehan has considerable capacity to continue its work in directing people's emotions and actions in positive ways, changing attitudes towards eliminating violence against women, promoting greater equity for women in society and strengthening the community base through popular and informal education that focuses specifically on building core values and principles for personal development and peaceful coexistence (Cox 2004b).

CONCLUSION

Cox's (2004b) evaluation of the SCP project illustrates clearly how much Leitana Nehan achieved over a few years. However, a great deal of humanitarian, human rights and social development work is yet to be completed in Bougainville to ensure that the region moves to a new era of autonomy. In other words, Leitana Nehan's violence-reduction work needs to be complemented by development opportunities that will help Bougainville establish a viable economy. Leitana Nehan's teams must also extend their outreach activities and violence-reduction work to the numerous villages of Bougainville that they could not reach within the SCP project's timeframe. Areas within the no-go zone and the western parts of Bougainville in particular will require assistance in forthcoming years. Much of this work will involve counselling and violence-awareness workshops.

Regarding Leitana Nehan and its future development activities, three support programs under SCP showed great potential for further development. These include the radio program, which worked well in disseminating information and complementing the organisation's outreach activities; the counselling service, which was able to deal with hidden but sensitive violence issues in society; and the theatre troupe, which was able to reach people in the community who may not have otherwise come forward to report particular incidents of violence against women and children. These programs worked in concert to consolidate the teams' activities.[8]

The second phase of the SCP project concentrated much time in engaging with government agencies, community leaders and other local and international civil society organisations to reduce violence in society. In addition, Leitana Nehan was actively involved in promoting women's role as leaders and politicians in support of 'good governance' in Bougainville during the autonomy period. It also paid careful attention to planning for its future as an NGO by developing a strategic plan and writing project proposals that built on their strengths following SCP (LNWDA 2003b, 2004). The SCP project could function as a springboard for Leitana Nehan, helping it launch new projects and carry on the peace-building work commenced during SCP, which provided experience in project management and implementation as well as in the delivery of desired social outcomes in the context of post-conflict recovery.

Ultimately, the success of Phase 2 lies in the extent to which local communities have gained the capacity to address their social problems independently, organise themselves to secure funds, and gain skills through local CBOs. Many of the case study communities in Phase 2 were moving in this positive direction. A mechanism to support these new CBOs for several years following their establishment would be useful, and this is a role that Leitana Nehan could continue to perform given sufficient funding. Furthermore, the work that Leitana Nehan has commenced in local communities during SCP needs to be extended to cover the majority of villages on Bougainville in order to avoid pockets of violence prevailing or spreading to other areas. Additional funding would enable this grassroots anti-violence movement to grow so that many more local communities in Bougainville can benefit from the peace-building activities undertaken by Leitana Nehan. The expectation is that more funding will be available during the period of autonomy to extend peace-building activities in the region. Peace-building is the necessary first step towards building community capacity for socioeconomic development in Bougainville. Little can be achieved without funds to implement projects such as SCP in order to set up the necessary peaceful preconditions for economic development.

NOTES

[1]   In terms of gender awareness, LNWDA sees a need for men to accept women as equal partners in all areas of development, in finding a lasting solution for peace and in ending the cycle of violence in Bougainville society following the crisis. The

organisation acknowledges the special place that women have in Bougainville, which is directly related to the matrilineal systems that exist in most parts of Bougainville (LNWDA and IWDA 2001).

[2] Leitana Nehan sent several of its staff for professional development training. For example, Kris Hakena participated in a non-violence and peacebuilding workshop in India (2001), and Bianca Hakena attended a counselling workshop (AWAYS) in Thailand (2002).

[3] For many and varied reasons, including distance, access and transport costs, it seemed relatively difficult for Leitana Nehan to work regularly in the western districts of Bougainville.

[4] Trainers from Fiji Women's Crisis Centre (FWCC) in Suva conducted a basic counselling skills workshop in Buka for 42 people in August 2003, providing an opportunity for a number of team counsellors and community leaders to gain basic training in counselling (LNWDA n.d.). Helen Hakena acted as a co-facilitator during this training. Funding for the counselling training in 2001 and 2003 came from New Zealand Aid rather than the SCP budget.

[5] The Peace March in Buka featured in two newspaper articles printed in the *Post-Courier* in Papua New Guinea. The first article on 10 November reported on the women's protests and the second article on 27 November was about the calls by Bougainville women to destroy weapons.

[6] Leitana Nehan was successful in gaining funding from New Zealand Aid for a follow-up to SCP, which concentrated solely on counselling. Again, Leitana Nehan has generated its next stage by building on the strengths of their previous experience.

[7] The executive director of Leitana Nehan, Helen Hakena, provides an ideal model of a woman leader. Ms Hakena was publicly supported by a male deputy, George Lesi, who had been the province's chief administrator in the past, and her husband, Kris Hakena, who is a prominent businessman and the chief of his clan on the island of Buka. Furthermore, many public servants and government officials supported her as well. These examples illustrate public respect for a woman leader and how women and men can work well in partnership.

[8] All of these support programs are active in the new SCP project that is underway.

6   GENDER, DEVELOPMENT AND PEACE

Peter Ninnes

The previous chapters have described Leitana Nehan's work over the last 12 years. We have attempted to show how the work conducted by the organisation has changed over time in response to the changing situation on the ground in Bougainville. We have also described the way the organisation has been able to build up the abilities and capacities of its staff and volunteers, and partner with a range of local, national and international organisations. In this and the following chapters we adopt a more analytical approach and attempt to explain in more detail the reasons why Leitana Nehan has been able to continue to grow and expand its work to a variety of social sites and institutions. There are many reasons for the Leitana Nehan's successful expansion and growing influence, including the social standing of its founders and their spouses, and of the volunteers, the commitment and hard work of its founders and subsequent staff and volunteers, the willingness of partners to contribute to the work, and the ability of the organisation to change and adapt to new circumstances. However, another major reason is the organisation's ability to take up, use, promote and gain acceptance for its vision for Bougainville, and particularly for its ideas about the role of women in Bougainville society, its vision of peace, and its ideas about development. In this chapter, therefore, I analyse how over time the organisation and its workers have conceptualised gender, development and peace, and how these conceptualisations have changed in response to changing contexts on Bougainville.

In essence I am exploring how Leitana Nehan's power operates. This is not a power that is oppressive or hierarchical; rather, as Foucault

(1991:194) observed, power is productive—'it produces reality; it produces domains of objects and rituals of truth'. In other words, it is through the operation of power that we come to understand and interpret the world and our place in it. Leitana Nehan's work in conveying particular ideas about women, peace and development therefore can be seen as a struggle to change the way people view the world, and in particular Bougainville, and their place in it. Most of this work of changing the way people view the world occurs through the use of language in particular contexts. Actions also have a major part to play by setting examples of how to behave. Nevertheless, the meanings of these actions are not transparent, but are explored and understood by and through language. In this chapter, therefore, i focus on language and in particular the discourses about women, development and peace that Leitana Nehan has used over time. Discourses are often the means through which power operates. Thus, they too are productive, since they 'systematically form the objects of which they speak' (Foucault 1972:49).

In the case of Leitana Nehan, these discourses have been deployed in two particular contexts, apart from the obvious ones of the crisis and its aftermath. The original founders of Leitana Nehan were already active in leadership roles in the Bougainville Diocese of the Catholic Women's Association prior to the conflict. Since the majority of Bougainville people are affiliated with the Catholic Church, these leadership roles and the CWA network provided a ready-made template on which to graft peace-building work. Second, and probably more fundamentally, Agnes, Helen, Brenda and Alina all hold chiefly positions in the social structure of their clans in Nissan and central, south and north Buka respectively. Thus they have respected and influential social connections throughout Nissan and Buka. Furthermore, within Bougainville societies, there are also chiefly connections across clans, and in some cases this meant that the Leitana Nehan founders had connections on the mainland of Bougainville as well. As I showed in Chapter 4, these connections were sometimes used to expand Leitana Nehan's work into various districts in Bougainville.

In the following analysis, I show how Leitana Nehan, through its founders and associates, has productively used, in the contexts described above, three sets of discourses around gender, development and peace. These deployments have for the most part been productive in the sense that they have allowed the organisation to recruit a growing cohort of volunteers; obtain approval to conduct their programs in a rising number of villages, schools and other social institutions; promote their work to, and create philosophical and financial partnerships with, a range of local, national and international organisations; and ensure women's issues are considered at various levels of the peace-building process, including disarmament talks and constitutional committee meetings. I analyse a range of official Leitana Nehan documents, as well as data from the interviews with Leitana Nehan founders, paid employees and volunteers.

WOMEN AND GENDER

Leitana Nehan has employed a range of the wide variety of discourses of gender that circulate globally and that have been identified by Tong (1998). In its first few years, Leitana Nehan tended to deploy culturally oriented discourses of gender that emphasised the important roles that Bougainville women have traditionally played in Bougainville societies. As Helen noted, the early emphasis was on improving family life. Mothers give birth to men and children. Since mothers are custodians of the land they are therefore leaders in improving family and community life. The purpose of using these discourses was to attempt to re-establish women's social roles, which had been eroded by colonialism prior to 1975, the mining operations and their associated social disruption (see also Wesley-Smith and Ogan 1992), and by the ten years of civil war.

In the mid 1990s, and particularly after two key members of the organisation, Helen Hakena and Agnes Titus, attended the International Women's Forum in Beijing in 1995, Leitana Nehan began to deploy liberal discourses of enhancing women's opportunities and protecting and promoting women's rights. This was partly a result of discussions that Helen and Agnes held with women in parishes on Buka, who decided 'women's rights' were compatible with what they needed. The women realised they needed to speak out (as was their right) because the men were *bagarap* (incapable) and too scared to speak.

These liberal discourses of women's rights are reflected in Leitana Nehan documents. For example, article 3.6.1 of the Leitana Nehan constitution (LNWDA 1997) states that one of the organisation's aims is

> [t]o promote, maintain and protect the interests, rights and privileges of the women of Bougainville irrespective of religion, colour, creed or affiliation.

The proposal submitted by Leitana Nehan and IWDA to AusAID for the Strengthening Communities for Peace project indicated that one of the proposed outputs would be 'increased awareness throughout Bougainville Province, Papua New Guinea and the Pacific about women's rights and concerns' (LNWDA and IWDA 1999:3). Similarly, the 2000 Annual Report notes that the overall goal of the SCP project is to 'contribute to the restoration of peace in Bougainville by promoting non-violence and women's rights' (LNWDA 2001a:10).

A promotional brochure produced in 2001 takes up the theme of women's rights, as well as indicating a concern with enhancing women's social standing.

> To meaningfully contribute to restoration of peace in Bougainville by promoting non-violence society and advocacy of women's rights. And also empowering women as agents of change and the improvement of their social status (LNWDA 2001b:n.p.)

Most recently, the Leitana Nehan strategic plan (LNWDA 2003a) identified the promotion of rights as one of its key strategic priorities, and in this case the discourse of women's rights has been extended to include children's rights. For example, the strategic plan (LNWDA 2003a) states that the organisation exists for 'the promotion of women and children's rights'. According to one of the monthly reports for the SCP project (LNWDA 2003b), one of the achievements of the project has been the inclusion of a statement on women's and children's rights in the draft constitution for an autonomous Bougainville.

Leitana Nehan also deployed a discourse focused on international conventions and national obligations to strengthen its claims concerning women's and children's rights. This is a practice that Chan-Tiberghien (2004) refers to as leverage politics. It involves using the ideas, status and standing of international conventions and declarations to lobby for change at the local level. The 1999 Annual Report, for example, stated

> Leitana Nehan in a small way carries out public awareness on the rights of women stipulated under the Papua New Guinea constitution and any other international laws and declarations issues under the United Nations charter (LNWDA 2000a:6).

Furthermore, the 2004–07 Strategic Plan (LNWDA 2003a:5) states that the organisation promotes these rights 'as stipulated in the Convention on all Forms of Violence against Women (CEDAW) and the Convention on the Rights of the Child (CRC)'.

Another impact of the Beijing forum was that Leitana Nehan openly eschewed certain elements of separatist radical feminist discourses (Tong 1998) that excluded men from contributing to the organisation's work. Rather, they argued that in Bougainville societies women, men and children work together, and therefore it would be inappropriate to adopt a separatist stance.[2] Furthermore, as one founder noted in the margin of the interview transcript which she proofread

> [i]f we confine gender issues to women only to deal with, then it will be seen as women's issues. But we are involving men to make them feel they are part of the issue and it is their issue, too. So the problems are community issues to be worked out together, by men and women.

Thus, in a submission to International Alert (LNWDA 2000b), Leitana Nehan stated: 'The issue on gender development has to be aggressively promoted to enable men and women [to] work hand in hand on issues and programmes affecting their lives'. Similarly, in the 2000 Annual Report (LNWDA 2001a:10), Leitana Nehan stated

> [t]here is a big need for men to see women as equal partners in all areas of development. Bougainville men and women need to work together hand in hand to find a lasting peaceful solution to the armed conflict on Bougainville.

Leitana Nehan also uses other cultural discourses of gender, particularly when lobbying for women's representation at disarmament talks and other public political forums that men attempt to dominate numerically. These cultural discourses argue that Bougainville women have a unique place in Bougainville societies and therefore particular roles to play in peace-making and post-conflict recovery. This is a form of what Tong (1998:47) calls a radical cultural feminism in which '[w]omen should not try to be like men…they should try to be more like women, emphasising the values and virtues culturally associated with women'. For example, in the SCP proposal

(LNWDA and IWDA 1999:5), the coordinator of Leitana Nehan was quoted as saying, 'Our women feel that their potential and capabilities in helping with rehabilitation and development need to be recognised because they hold important keys no one else can turn'. Similarly, in the 2000 Annual Report (LNWDA 2001a:10), Leitana Nehan argued, 'Women have a special place in the Bougainville society…as a result of the matrilineal system that existed on Bougainville'. The Leitana Nehan promotional brochure, also takes up this theme.

> We recognise and endeavour to build upon capacities of people to resolve their own conflicts and we support the distinctive peace making roles of women in societies affected by the violent conflict (LNWDA 2001b:n.p.).

In some contexts, such as international forums, Leitana Nehan deploys global feminist discourses, in which all women are viewed as part of a sisterhood, despite their differing experiences of oppression (Tong 1998:242). For example, in a speech in Melbourne marking International Women's Day in 2003, Helen Hakena (2003a) addressed her audience as 'sisters'.

DEVELOPMENT

In terms of development, there has been a shift in the emphasis that the organisation places on social, cultural and economic change. In its original form as a humanitarian relief organisation, Leitana Nehan provided clothes and medicine for women and children who had been moved from the war zones into 'care centres' by the PNG military (see Chapter 2). Later, the organisation began to emphasise development. For example the Leitana Nehan Constitution (LNWDA 1997:n.p.) states that one of the organisation's objectives is 'to work towards the improvement of the living standards of the women of Bougainville so as to enable them to achieve gradual economic and social development'. By the end of the 1990s, however, and with a truce in the war, Leitana Nehan began to emphasise integral human development (IHD), based on certain Catholic teachings that argue that economic and infrastructure development is premature without personal, spiritual and moral development. For example, in the SCP proposal, one of the major activity outputs was to be 'a mutually supportive network formed of 120 community representatives able to work with their communities in an ongoing fashion using IHD principles to address social problems' (LNWDA and IWDA 1999:3). The same document gave a detailed description and rationale for IHD.

> IHD provides a holistic approach to community development that highlights the inter-relatedness of social problems. The IHD workshops will explore the wide range of factors that cause violence and disharmony in the community, including, anger, grief, fear, trauma and lack of self understanding, lack of self worth and insufficient guidance/direction for young people...the workshops will aim to equip the community representatives with the tools to facilitate psychological, emotional and spiritual rehabilitation, and to motivate communities to creatively address social problems (LNWDA and IWDA 1999:10).

This illustrates the priority given to non-material development as a prerequisite for economic and physical development. Other documents provide further insight into the reasons for this priority. For example, the 1999 Annual Report (LNWDA 2000a:1) states that IHD is a priority because 'many Bougainvilleans were traumatised and suffered a lot during the ninth [sic] year armed conflict on Bougainville'. Furthermore, the 2000 Annual Report (LNWDA 2001a:1) states, 'the focus on Integral Human Development must be given priority in order for Unity, Peace and Development to prosper on Bougainville'. Leitana Nehan tends to view IHD as 'people-centred development'. In its promotional brochure (LNWDA 2001b:n.p.), it states, 'above everything else, men, women and children of Bougainville shall be at the centre of any form of development politically, economically, socially, spiritually and culturally'. Most recently, the organisation's strategic plan has continued to emphasise holistic development.

> The organisation will practise a holistic approach to development that encompasses physical, spiritual, social and economic well being. Leitana Nehan believes that each person deserves an opportunity to develop, to the fullest possible extent, his or her own physical, mental, emotional and spiritual potential (LNWDA 2003a:5).

> For several years, Leitana Nehan has promoted integral human development as a prerequisite to economic and infrastructure development. We believe that any form of development should improve the quality of life for all Bougainvilleans (LNWDA 2003a:3).

It is noteworthy that in both of the above passages, there is a shift from the 1997 constitution, which focused solely on women's development. In the 2004–07 Strategic Plan, the vision has expanded to improving the quality of life for all Bougainvilleans.

Many of the interviewees subscribed to the integral human development model. When asked what development was, they mentioned ideas such as assisting people to know and understand themselves and relate to others; developing respect for other people; that development had mental, physical, spiritual and social dimensions; that it involved the whole person; creating good people; changing attitudes and behaviours, including one's own; decreasing the number of troublemakers; and ridding the community of bad things such as homebrew, domestic violence and child abuse. One interviewee suggested that development was about training and informing the public about issues, providing opportunities to debate issues, and knowing the differences between various approaches to dealing with specific issues. Some interviewees, when defining integral human development, contrasted it with models that focused only on infrastructure, such as buildings, schools, bridges and rainwater tanks. One interviewee, however, argued that development did involve 'schools, trade stores and providing services to the people'. One interviewee argued it was no use building schools and clinics if people were in the frame of mind to burn them down, which is what happened during the war, and therefore it was important to deal with the psychological trauma of the war before re-establishing infrastructure. According to another interviewee, reconciliation as well as psychological healing is necessary so that people trust each other and can work together to improve their lives. This interviewee cited two instances in which an outside aid organisation had implemented programs before adequate levels of reconciliation and healing had occurred. In one case, the program had sapped people's initiative and led to a hand-out mentality, while in the other case it had made people suspicious of the aid organisation's local partner, with the result that the local partner had to work hard to allay these fears.

Some of the interviewees who advocated IHD also argued that development involved employment generation projects, such as those that supplied sewing machines, ovens or seeds, or provided for the creation of other small businesses. There was a sense that people needed to be gainfully employed so that they did not go back to making homebrew and causing trouble. One interviewee also observed that such projects worked best when focused on the extended family, rather than the whole community.

The source of a substantial proportion of Leitana Nehan's ideas on IHD is a book by a Catholic Priest, Father Tony Byrne (1983), which focuses on 'integral development', although in the Leitana Nehan documents the work 'human' is inserted in the phrase. Byrne (1983:6) cites Pope Paul VI's 1967 book, *The Development of Peoples*, which defines development as the 'promotion of the good of people, every person and the whole person', rather than the development of material things such as buildings. The book promotes a consultative, participatory model of development, and advises against paternalistic approaches. At the same time, it treats the question of gender equality dismissively, as evidenced by the following anecdote.

> Some time ago I asked a group of people attending a development seminar to draw their idea of development. One Sister who was attending the seminar had a good sense of humour. She drew a picture of a Sister wearing a bishop's mitre ... I suppose we will have to wait for some time before we have that kind of development! (Byrne 1983:6).

Yet the 2004–07 Strategic Plan makes it quite clear that Leitana Nehan itself highly values gender equality.

> The promotion of gender equality is an underlying principle of the organisation…The organisation will promote and practise equal participation by women and men in all aspects of Leitana Nehan operations. It is important that the organisation serve as a role model of gender equity (LNWDA 2003:5).

This is an example of the way in which Leitana Nehan selectively appropriates discourses of development and gender that they consider useful to them at particular points in time. Further examples are found in recent documents, which consecutively take up three other development discourses. First, starting in the late 1990s, Leitana Nehan used a discourse of empowerment. Initially, the focus was on the empowerment of women. The SCP proposal (LNWDA and IWDA 1999:3) aims to have 'women around Buka and Bougainville Islands empowered by access to counselling, basic legal advice and referrals to lawyers to extricate themselves from abusive domestic situations'. Similarly, the 2001 promotional brochure states (LNWDA 2001b) that Leitana Nehan has the aim of 'empowering women as agents of change and the improvement of their social status'. Yet Leitana Nehan also argues for broader levels of empowerment. The 2000 Annual Report argues, 'youth empowerment is the key to Youth Development on Bougainville' (LNWDA 2001a:11). The 2004–07 Strategic Plan (LNWDA 2003a:5) also recommends empowerment for the population in general, since 'empowering communities and their organisations' is one of the five strategic areas in the plan, and 'Leitana Nehan recognises that people have the right to organise in pursuit of their own interests and should be empowered to define and lead their own development efforts'.

Several of the interviewees mentioned these kinds of ideas when discussing development. One of the Leitana Nehan founders said development involved 'empowering women to be agents of change', while one volunteer said development meant 'developing women to exercise their rights', as well as helping men to understand women's rights and not think of them as servants or slaves. One of Leitana Nehan's project officers said that development involves making women aware of their rights and of where to get help when they need it, and to involve women in decision-making.

Second, the discourse on capacity-building appears around about the year 2000. The 2000 Annual Report describes workshops that had been run that year to 'build capacity' of Buka youth (LNWDA 2001a:9) and Siwai women (LNWDA 2001a:11), while similar workshops were run in 2001 for Buka women (LNWDA 2002a:5). The current strategicplan also deploys this discourse, particularly with respect to the organisation itself, which lists '[s]trengthening the capacity and sustainability of LNWDA' as one of its five strategic areas (LNWDA 2003a:1). None of the interviewees specifically mentioned capacity-building, although one team leader did mention that development involved increasing people's skills in areas such as business management.

A third and more recent development discourse focuses on 'good governance'. This discourse first appears in the title and content of the 2004–07 Strategic Plan (LNWDA 2003a). One of the strategic areas in the plan is 'practising good governance', while a goal of the plan is '[t]o promote good governance within the organisation and in our relationships with key stakeholders' (LNWDA 2003a:15). Among other things this is to be done by having 'appropriate policies and procedures…in place to ensure accountability and transparency' (LNWDA 2003a:15). Although good governance appears as a discourse in official documents, none of the interviewees mentioned it specifically as a component of development.

Some interviewees identified a cultural component to development, which had two dimensions. First, some interviewees saw development as involving a return to the lifestyle or customs that existed before the war. For two interviewees, development meant moving towards attaining *sindaun bilong bifo* (life in the past), in which traditional customs were followed such as sharing, speaking properly, respect, working together and not fighting. For one of these interviewees, development also meant reducing the impact of custom on women's rights. Second, one interviewee noted that development projects have to be compatible with, and fit in with, ceremonial schedules. For example, participants in a development project should observe the ten-day mourning period after a funeral and obtain permission from the chiefs before recommencing work.

PEACE

Like the discourses of gender and development, the discourses of peace employed by Leitana Nehan have shifted in response to the changing situation in Bouganville. The Leitana Nehan constitution (LNWDA 1997), which was developed at about the same time that the 1997 truce came into effect, lists as objectives of the organisation 'women's integration into the reconciliation, reconstruction and rehabilitation process of Bougainville' (article 3.4) and 'to assist and partake in the peace process of Bougainville thus ensuring that normalcy returns to Bougainville' (article 3.10). The former article in particular indicates an emphasis on participating in three of the major tasks of post-conflict recovery. The triumvirate of reconciliation, reconstruction and rehabilitation has persisted into the discourse in the current strategic plan, with an acknowledgement of the inter-linked contributions of a range of actors at various social levels.

> Bougainville is now on the road to recovery. We are in the process of rebuilding our lives and restoring essential services. Reconstruction, reconciliation and rehabilitation are people's highest priority. Peace-building programs are being implemented in all areas on Bougainville, supported by communities and assisted by churches, NGOs, the government and international aid agencies (LNWDA 2003a:4).

The SCP proposal (LNWDA and IWDA 1999) shifts the 'peace' emphasis from the crisis, which effectively finished in terms of armed conflict in 1998, to violence in general and against women in particular when it argues that the overall goal of the project is to 'contribute to the restoration of peace in Bougainville by promoting non-violence and women's rights' (LNWDA and IWDA 1999:6). Identical wording is used in the SCP Year 2 annual plan (LNWDA and IWDA 2001:4). Reconciliation was a particular aim of the youth mobilisations described in Chapter 3. The 2000 Annual Report reflects this when it states that one of the aims of the Tinputz youth mobilisation was to 'bring together youth as a means of promoting peace, unity and reconciliation among youth' (LNWDA 2001a:9). In addition to reconciliation, the organisation has emphasised emotional and psychological healing as an important component of the peace-building process.

> Weapons can be containerised and disposed of, expensive infrastructure can be built, with assurance of a better and brighter future by leaders. However, peace will be just a dream if people's minds are not healed (Hakena 2003a:n.p.).

The discourses of gender and peace intersect. In particular, the radical culturalist feminist discourse that identifies unique social and cultural roles for women, described above, is employed to explain the role of women in both peace-making and post-conflict recovery.

> It was the women who risked going out into the jungle to persuade our sons, husbands and brothers to avert war. It was the women who really made peace, not

the menfolk. They were busy killing, destroying and raping women (Hakena 2003a:n.p.).

> Women are not passive victims. We are contributing actively to peace-making. Our courage and contributions have made the world a better place to live and work. Imagine what more we could do if we women were enabled to take a more equal place at the negotiating table (Hakena 2003a:n.p.).

The volunteers and staff members interviewed for this study defined peace in terms of particular absences and presences. The most common definition, mentioned by nine respondents, was that peace means to have a good life, to *stap gut* or have a *gutpela sindaun*. Six respondents said that peace meant 'freedom', which is not surprising because during the war freedom of movement was curtailed, with many displaced persons in the government-controlled areas confined to care centres and those behind the BRA lines unable to cross the blockade (see Sirivi and Havini 2004). Three or less respondents mentioned other components of peace, including contentment, satisfaction, respect for others, respect for property, abiding by the law, peace *(bel isi)*, reconciliation, cooperation between people, loving each other, living as one, listening to chiefs, being happy *(amamas)*, enjoying life, respect for traditional values, having basic needs met, being settled, and *brukim bonara, wokem bikfala kaikai, wokem lotu* (that is, the traditional peace-making rituals of breaking weapons, having a feast and a church service—see Howley 2002; Fisher 2004).

In terms of absences, there were a wide variety of responses. The most common were that peace involved an absence of violence (four respondents), war (three respondents), fighting (two respondents), threats (two respondents), fear (two respondents), and harassment (two respondents). Individual respondents also mentioned an absence of danger, disturbances, discrimination against women, retaliation, trouble, the desire to kill, problems *(hevi)*, stealing, use of weapons, land disputes, hatred and alcohol-related crime.

In general, the respondents showed an understanding of peace that went beyond simplistic definitions of peace as the absence of war. In particular, there was an emphasis on the quality of life, both for individuals and for groups. A similar level of sophistication was displayed concerning respondents' understanding of the causes of peace. A common response was that peace begins with a change in one's own perspective. One respondent said that 'a change in people is needed; a transformation to respect others as oneself'. Another said that 'peace grows from within us…realising what I've done wrong to the other person'. A third person said that peace was the result of *lustingting olsem pait, stil* (forget about doing things like fighting and stealing). A fourth said that peace was the result of a spiritual change, while a fifth said that peace involved 'rehabilitation of the minds of the people'. The heart was considered by a number of respondents to be a locus for initiating peace: 'it has to come from the bottom of your heart', and 'genuine peace comes through the heart' were two responses. Alternatively, families were considered by some respondents to be a starting point for peace-making. One respondent said peace 'must start with the family', while another said that 'children must respect parents *na tok tok gud long famle* [and speak respectfully to family members] in order to make a different community'.

A number of respondents argued that, once individuals were at peace with themselves, this would have a flow-on effect. One respondent said *Emi stat long ol wan wan man na emi save go long famle na long ples* (it [peace] starts with individuals, then spreads to the family and community). Another said, 'we have to produce peace in ourselves, then the family, community, district and province'.

For some respondents, the spreading of peace described above was not inevitable, but required actions such as cooperation, a collective effort, hard work, reconciliation, forgiveness and trust-building. One respondent suggested that it is necessary to reconcile, admit failures, give compensation and return stolen property. Another respondent indicated faith in traditional methods: 'not just shaking hands, but killing a pig and giving it, witnessed by the chiefs'. On the other hand, two respondents were sceptical of the efficacy of traditional reconciliation methods. One said peace is 'just a handshake and a feast. That's superficial and won't last…[we] need to address all the unfinished issues such as polygamy, stealing, adultery, domestic violence'. Another said, 'reconciliation feasts won't work if it doesn't come from the heart'.

While most of the respondents saw peace as a process that involved individuals, family and community transformation, only one respondent took a more external, political view that reflected some of the issues that provoked the Bougainville crisis. He argued that *sipos jastis emi kamap bai pis emi kamap* (if there is justice, then there will be peace)', and that if independence comes, then peace will come.

A number of respondents discussed the consequences of peace when defining peace and its causes. Apart from general comments about making communities better places to live, six respondents mentioned that peace meant that health and education services could be available, and other development work could be done. During the blockade, these kinds of services were difficult or impossible to maintain (see Sirivi and Havini 2004), and one of the major arguments used to promote the peace process and to encourage reluctant ex-combatants to join has been the promise of the so-called peace dividend, namely improvement of living conditions and restoration of services (see, for example, Barter 2004). One of the founders' spouses developed this point by remarking that peace-building was not just about reconstructing the economy, but also about reconstructing morals and culture.

NOTES

[1] Interview, Helen Hakena, 19 February 2004.
[2] Interview, Helen Hakena, 19 February 2004.

7 PARTNERSHIP, POST-CONFLICT DEVELOPMENT AND PEACE-BUILDING

Jonathan Makuwira

In the study and practice of development, the concept of partnerships has been both pervasive and contested. In this chapter I analyse partnerships in post-conflict development and peace-building from four perspectives, using Leitana Nehan as a case study. The first section of the chapter explores the concept of partnership, the various theoretical perspectives related to the notion of partnership, and common types and models of partnerships. The second section describes the kinds of partnerships Leitana Nehan has engaged in, based on the various models described. The third and concluding section of the chapter analyses the strengths and weaknesses of partnership-building approaches. It summarises key issues emerging from this analysis and provides a reflection on the theory and practice of partnerships in development and peace-building.

PARTNERSHIP IN CONTEXT

Currently, there is overwhelming agreement that development, poverty eradication, and peace-building can best be achieved through establishing partnerships both at the national and international levels. The discourse of partnership dominates many major international and national development declarations and instruments. For example, the UN Millennium Development Goals (MDGs), Education for Sustainable Development, and UNESCO's International Year for the Culture of Peace stipulate the importance of establishing partnerships as a means to achieving other objectives. However, while partnership-building sounds rosy and optimistic in theory, the concept of partnership is difficult to implement in practice. There is no level playing field in partnership-building because the concept is political, and the participating organisations may have their own agendas that create imbalance.

The change in the nature, size, value, mission and objectives of many development organisations, both from the North and the South[1], especially with regard to development and aid, has resulted in the adoption of the concept of partnership. As Fowler (1991) contends, the concept of partnership has, since the 1970s, been widely used and given multiple meanings. It is often used synonymously with 'relationship'. Lewis (2001) adds that the term is used interchangeably with 'collaboration', 'coordination', 'cooperation', 'accompaniment', and 'complementarity', which he says have entrenched themselves in development discourse. Originally, the concept of partnership was used and understood to reflect humanitarian, moral, political, ideological or spiritual solidarity between the northern NGOs and those from the South, who also shared a common vision—facilitating social change.

In its basic form, the term 'partnership' means a strategic alliance or coalition between two or more entities that are involved in pursuing a particular issue but share resources and responsibilities in order to achieve a common goal (Fowler 1997). Fowler (2000b, in Brehm 2001:11) further extends this definition from the perspective of whether such partnerships are authentic or not. He argues that, 'authentic partnership implies...a joint commitment to long-term intervention, shared responsibility for achievement, reciprocal obligation, equality, mutuality and balance of power'.

Lewis (2001) critiques the absence of proper scrutiny of how the concept of partnership works in the development and aid arena. He notes that the lack of balanced partnerships has resulted in a complex dichotomy, where those involved can become active or passive partners. As Fowler (2000a:26) argues, 'the phrase "partnership in development" has become virtually meaningless and discredited because too often it camouflages aid-related relationships that are unbalanced, dependency-creating and based on compromise in favour of the powerful'. For example, Fowler observes that the dependency and power imbalance can be exacerbated by, among other things, donors imposing conditionality that undermines NGOs' governance, accountability, comparative advantages, organisational behaviour and focus.

The various facets of these definitions contain a number of underlying assumptions, which form the fundamental ingredients of an effective partnership. Whether these partnerships are in form of coalitions, alliances or networks, Fowler (2000c) and Lewis (2001) argue that effective partnerships or relationships are anchored in mutuality. It is also vital to note that those involved in the partnership have an important part to play as equals while maintaining their organisational independence.

TYPES AND MODELS OF PARTNERSHIPS

Analysts of aid and development (see Leach 1997; INTRAC 2001; Fowler 2000c; Tvedt 1998; Martinussen and Engberg-Pedersen 2003) have formulated various models of partnerships to reflect the complexity of these interplays between the two entities. My focus will be on the following kinds of partnerships

- NGO–donor
- Inter-NGO
- NGO–government
- NGO–local community.

NGO–donor agency partnership

It is widely acknowledged that the study of partnerships should focus on the dynamics of power (Lister 1999). According to Lister, many theories of power are behavioural, largely concerned with the extent to which the actions of one organisation can have such a significant influence on the behaviour of the other organisation. Given that the aid and development industry is based on resource transfer, one question whose answer remains elusive is the extent to which Northern and Southern NGOs are really partners in a reciprocally accountable relationship. Many partnerships are believed to be founded on a shared vision, hence, the common 'visionary patronage' model of partnership; others are based on desires or needs for collaboration; while still other partnerships focus on resources, capacity enhancement and/or mutual trust. I discuss each of these in turn below.

Visionary Patronage Model

According to Leach (1997:6) visionary patronage is a partnership where an international NGO (or a consortium of international NGOs) collaborates with a local or national NGO (or consortium of NGOs) on the basis of a strong, shared development goal or vision. Leitana Nehan and International Women's Development Agency reflect this model in many respects. For example, Leitana Nehan's vision aims to 'meaningfully contribute to the restoration of peace on Bougainville by promoting non-violence and women's rights and empowering women as agents of change to improve their social status' (Carl 2000:10). Likewise, IWDA's vision seeks to 'support women's efforts to improve their life and choices and those of their families and communities, and to advance women's human rights, with emphasis on women who are particularly marginalised or suffer poverty or oppression' (IWDA n.d.). The emphasis on the improvements of women's social status underlines the argument. While the emphasis is on the vision, there is no obligation for shared strategy. What is common in this model of collaboration is joint formulation of goals for specific project activities, the monitoring of outcomes and reporting. Very often though, partners in a visionary patronage model of partnership have had a working relationship before. In the case of IWDA and Leitana Nehan, the two organisations established this collaborative partnership prior to the NGO forum in Beijing in 1995 (see Chapter 2) and consolidated it through a joint project, which was later funded by the Australian government, through AusAID (see Chapters 4 and 5).

Funding, capacity and trust

In addition to the visionary patronage and collaborative relationships between NGOs and donors, these relationships can also be further conceptualised in terms of

- funding-based differences, with 'a funding-only relationship at one end of the spectrum and a partnership based on policy dialogue with no funding at the other end' (INTRAC 2001:3)

- capacity-based differences, ranging from an NGO with limited capacity to implement programs on its own at one extreme, to an NGO that is self-sufficient in terms of resources and experience at the other
- trust-based differences, ranging from the situation where one partner, usually the one with resources, takes total control of the recipient NGO, to a situation of unconditional trust between the two (INTRAC 2001).

Inter-NGO partnerships

Partnerships between and among NGOs vary. In some instances, they can take the form of temporary alliances, coalitions or simple platforms (Fowler 2000b). Some inter-NGO partnerships can be formal and legally established. One such example is NGO partnerships formed under umbrella or NGO-coordinating organisations. In this section, I critically examine inter-NGO partnerships from three perspectives. First, I look at the partnerships between Northern and Southern NGOs. Second, I examine inter-NGO partnerships within NGO coordinating bodies and, third, partnerships arising from networks and coalitions.

The North–South divide

Brehm (2001) contends that partnerships between Northern and Southern NGOs have become an important aspect in the development process. However, while Southern NGOs have been coerced into the concept of partnership, the practical aspects of the concept are not only complex but are also hotly contested. Too often, inter-NGO partnerships are largely driven by aid-related issues, which ultimately result in patron–client relationships. According to Fowler (2000b), when Southern NGOs fall into such partnerships with Northern NGOs, it is usually the Northern NGOs that impose their external development models and policies and the Southern NGOs are coerced into following them, raising the question of who owns the funds. Further imbalance in resources often results in what Nwamuo (2000) calls 'senior partners' who erode the aspect of ownership. Under such conditions, the Northern NGOs tend to control and determine priorities, budgets and activities, and this ultimately interferes with the autonomy of the local institutions.

Inter-NGO partnerships in NGO umbrella organisations

Over the years, the dynamics of NGO partnerships have taken a different dimension with many umbrella organisations formed to facilitate coordination in response to rampant tensions among NGOs. Korten (1990) recounts that 'jealousies among them are often intense, and efforts at collaboration too often break down into internecine warfare that paralyses efforts to work together towards the achievement of shared purposes. Ironically, it at times seems easier for some to work with government than with other NGOs' (1990:130–31).

Locally mandated frameworks or government-legislated NGO coordinating bodies are proving to be useful structures, although in some countries they are seen to interfere with NGO's independence. Such partnerships are not without problems. Bennet (1997) argues that they work best when they have both local and foreign support and they do not duplicate the functions of the member NGOs unless such duplication is specifically sought. Bennet further maintains that the effectiveness of NGO coordinating bodies may also depend on forming other network structures such as sector networks. In addition, he observes that these coordinating organisations should be endorsed by governments and other civil society actors as interlocutors on issues affecting the NGO sector. How member NGOs comply with codes of conduct devised by NGO coordinating bodies is another contentious issue.

Coalitions and networks

Networks have become fashionable in NGO partnerships. A conglomerate of NGOs may team up and form coalitions for various purposes, for example, advancing a policy reform issue. A number of UN summits have witnessed such networks or coalitions at work (Fisher 1993). Such coalitions and networks usually operate on a common interest and agenda, with a particular theme as their focus. For example, the Alliance for the Advancement of People's Rights, Bougainville Interchurch Women's Forum, and Women's International League for Peace and Freedom, are among many such networks.

NGO–government partnerships

One of the fundamental aspects of NGOs' success in their development efforts in general, and their peace-building endeavours in post-conflict situations in particular, is their relationship with the state (see Ropers 2001; Galama and van Tongeren 2002). State collapse in conflict situations causes complex challenges for reconstruction, which vary with context and the degree of state failure. For example, the conflict in Bougainville had such a devastating effect because it was an internal conflict, weakening the judicial, fiscal and administrative structures, and hence the possibilities for NGO partnerships important to the reconstruction process.

Identifying the partnership models that best facilitate sustainable development and peace-building in post-conflict situations is a complex issue, rendered even more difficult by NGOs' inability to establish meaningful partnerships with government given the absence of appropriate institutional structures. However, depending on the ceasefire mechanisms, there are ways in which dialogue can be initiated between civil society organisations and the government structures. As such, it is vital to explore what the literature says about the NGO–government partnership models in general, before identifying which models Leitana Nehan adopts in its projects.

Commentators on the NGO–government partnership discourse (see Gidron et al. 1992) suggest that there are four types of government–NGO partnerships: the government-dominant model, the third-sector dominant model, the dual model, and the collaborative model.

Government-dominant model. This model is characterised by the government's leading role in both the funding and delivery of services. Where possible, however, the NGO sector is contracted to deliver services on the government's behalf. Post-conflict situations may not always fit into this category. Nevertheless, as the role of the NGO sector becomes increasingly vital in post-conflict situations, their engagement could facilitate reconciliation and community mobilisation.

Third-sector dominant model. The major feature in this model is the dominant role played by the NGO both in the funding and delivery of services. This model is common in post-conflict situations where government services are limited or non-existent. Very often, NGOs will seek funding, identify needs, implement, monitor and evaluate their programs with very little or no government participation.

Dual model. As opposed to the two models above, the NGOs in a dual model, also known as the 'parallel track' model (Tvedt 1998:5), supplement the services provided by the state and deliver similar kinds of services. One distinguishing strategy is clear, however—in a 'dual model', NGOs give priority to the communities that are marginalised by state service provision, adopting the primary role of filling the gaps left by the government.

Collaborative model. One of the most conducive models, and perhaps one that strikes a balance, is the collaborative model. This model allows for the two sectors—government and NGOs—to work together. In this model, NGOs can act as agents of government programs (collaborative-vendor model) or, alternatively, can retain a considerable amount of autonomy and direction (collaborative-partnership model) (Tvedt 1998). The extent to which NGOs in post-conflict situations adopt this model largely depends on the stability of the post-conflict situation, particularly whether or not structures are in place to facilitate dialogue between and among different parties.

However, as can be deduced from the four models above, it is extremely difficult to pinpoint which model can work best in a given situation. The framework of relationships within which NGOs operate may vary from country to country. It is possible that a single model or a combination of two models or more can be adopted. As alluded to earlier, it may depend on the prevailing social, political, economic and cultural climate of the day.

NGO–local community partnerships

NGO relationships with local communities can be understood from the perspective of the extent to which NGOs engage local community members in their projects, that is, how the local people participate in NGO programs. Going back to the fundamental principles that govern both participatory development and effective partnerships (Fowler 1997, 2000a, 2000c), it can be deduced that both participation and partnerships are effective where there is high degree of information/resource sharing, consultation and decision-making, and where beneficiaries initiate action. Therefore, effective NGO–local community partnerships can be realised where NGO programs provide feedback to the beneficiaries or where consultation between the two is not a one-sided process but stems from mutual trust. Second, unless the beneficiaries are involved in the decision-making process on issues that affect them, partnership is more likely to fail.

LEITANA NEHAN'S ROAD TO BUILDING PARTNERSHIPS

Since its inception, Leitana Nehan has been engaged in various forms of partnerships with other stakeholders. While these partnerships seem discrete, they overlap in their fundamental principles and can be placed in the four broad categories discussed above, namely, NGO–donor, Inter-NGO, NGO–government, and NGO–local community. Leitana Nehan has had a long-standing partnership with the International Women's Development Agency (IWDA), an organisation predominantly funded by AusAID. As noted in Chapter 2, IWDA and Leitana Nehan first came into contact when IWDA sent Rae Smart and Sharon Laura to the 'Bougainville Reunion' in 1994. IWDA then sponsored two of Leitana Nehan's founders, Agnes Titus and Helen Hakena, to attend the Fourth Global Forum on Women in Beijing in 1995, allowing Leitana Nehan to put itself on the global stage for the first time by openly sharing with other participants Bougainville women's experiences in the conflict. The immediate effect of the Beijing forum was the establishment of a formal partnership with International Women's Development Agency. The partnership, however, reflects a set of sub-models, particularly Leach's (1997) 'visionary patronage' and 'collaborative operation'.

It is no coincidence that IWDA and Leitana Nehan share a fairly similar vision of women's role in peace-building and development, which underpins the collaboration. Both organisations focus on improving women's social status, among other fundamental issues.

As already alluded to earlier in the chapter, Leitana Nehan's partnership-building with other stakeholders, particularly AusAID and the International Women's Development Agency in Australia, New Zealand Aid and Oxfam New Zealand, were engineered by the organisation's vision, which is to 'meaningfully contribute to the restoration of peace on Bougainville by promoting non-violence and women's rights and empowering women as agents of change to improve their social status' (Carl 2000:10). This ambitious vision, in essence, meant embarking on a rigorous campaign to establish meaningful networks and funding, both from within Bougainville and the international donor community.

IWDA's intermediary role in the partnership

The pursuit of the visionary patronage model of partnership (within the broader context of the NGO–donor partnership) between AusAID and IWDA on the one hand, and between IWDA and Leitana Nehan on the other, is unique and has particular strengths and weaknesses. IWDA is a direct recipient of AusAID funding. In theory, Leitana Nehan has, to a large extent, been in a visionary patronage model of partnership with AusAID due to its (AusAID's) mandate to assist its recipients to reduce poverty and achieve sustainable development. In terms of funding mechanisms, however, Leitana Nehan is an indirect recipient—IWDA is the conduit through which funds are channelled. According to AusAID (n.d.) all Australian aid is supposed to 'promote the Australian identity', and that the role of the intermediary organisations (like IWDA) is to be 'responsible for the design, delivery, monitoring, and evaluation of the activities, submission of reports and acquittals, and for fully accounting for funds provided by AusAID' (AusAID n.d.:n.p.). This 'tied aid' policy potentially posed significant problems for the partnership between IWDA and Leitana Nehan. Two fundamental questions arise from this. Who benefits from these visionary partnerships? Who owns the aid package?

In theory, the visionary patronage model of partnership provides the flexibility for the maintenance of organisational identity. In practice, however, there are contradictions. In the case of the partnership between IWDA and Leitana Nehan, the contradiction is clearly seen in the conditions attached to the aid package. These conditions interfere with the many advantages which the visionary patronage partnership are supposed to provide, such as

- frequent visits
- exchange of information through reports
- mutual learning, particularly of the international NGO, and its ripple effects to other related projects
- enhanced learning by the recipient NGO in program strategy and financial management
- adaptability in project implementation, monitoring and evaluation.

Conversely, the visionary patronage model of partnership has a number of disadvantages both to the donor agency and recipient NGO. As Makuwira (2003) points out, the fact that donor agencies and other international NGOs (acting as conduits for donor agencies) are not fully engaged in the day-to-day operation of the project results in a significant loss of learning. Every development project produces lessons for improved practice. Furthermore, partnerships are highly embedded with elements of power. Where the recipient NGOs fail to articulate their mission and strategy clearly, they risk being swallowed by donor influences. Leitana Nehan has to deal with two critical issues, directly or indirectly—first, finding appropriate balance in its relationship with IWDA and, second, dealing with AusAID's influence on IWDA, which has the potential to affect Leitana Nehan's work. These issues are discussed later in the chapter.

COLLABORATIVE OPERATION

When partnerships are established on the basis of shared vision, expectations of collaboration are usually high. The challenge, however, lies in determining the degree of collaboration. Leach (1997) believes that the donor agency is supposed, under the collaborative operation partnership model, to be actively engaged in the governance of the project along with the recipient NGO. This model emphasises joint decision-making power during the project's design, implementation, monitoring and evaluation phases. Unlike the visionary patronage model, the collaborative operation model of partnership emphasises shared agreement on vision and strategy, a condition that usually requires some kind of formal decision-making structure.

The partnership between Leitana Nehan and IWDA does, to a certain degree, reflect this description. During the 2003 International Women's Day Conference held in Hobart, Helen Hakena, the director of the Leitana Nehan provided some background which supports the view that IWDA and Leitana Nehan have been engaged, to a larger extent, in a collaborative operation model of partnership. In her speech she said pointed out that

> [i]n 1994 International Women's Development Agency came to our aid, sending Ms Rae Smart and Sharon Laura to work with us during the peak of the crisis, to document the experiences of Bougainville women in the lead up to the Beijing World Forum on Women. This was the beginning of our valuable partnership with IWDA. In 1998 both organisations jointly devised a project called 'Strengthening Communities for Peace' (Hakena 2003a:3).

The frequent presence of IWDA staff at Leitana Nehan's office proved advantageous in many ways. Leitana Nehan has enjoyed a relatively long period of substantial funding from AusAID through IWDA. Not only has the relationship provided Leitana Nehan direct access to IWDA's expertise and staff experience, it has also allowed the organisation's staff to learn useful administrative and management skills, acquire knowledge of the politics of donor agencies and aid provision, and develop skills in fundraising and advocacy. Leitana Nehan has used all these skills very successfully in influencing policymaking in Bougainville. For example, Leitana Nehan, like other Bougainville local NGOs, has been in the forefront in contributing to the development of the Bougainville Constitution and other related activities (see Chapters 2–5).

There are also advantages to the partner international NGO (IWDA), most notably, lower staff costs and overheads, increased institutional effectiveness and opportunity for the agency to work in situations where direct operations are highly restricted, increased understanding of on-the-ground realities; and, in the case of IWDA, greater credibility with AusAID as an organisation that is willing to learn from its operations. For example, IWDA continues to receive support from AusAID, arguably not just because it satisfies many of

AusAID's requirements but because it shows a keen interest in pursuing mutual working partnerships.

The central dilemma, as is the case with visionary patronage, is where the parties involved draw the line between joint decision-making and interference. This partnership can be 'too close for comfort' because, if the donor agency or international NGO wields too much power and is insensitive to the needs of the beneficiary NGO, the beneficiary NGO risks losing control of its identity, culture, mission and strategy. This is probably the reason why many NGOs have fallen prey to donor agencies' conditionalities. Although this may be very hard to detect in the case of IWDA and Leitana Nehan, it is hard, given that IWDA is directly answerable and responsible to AusAID, to claim that IWDA and Leitana Nehan are operating on a level playing field.

Funding-based differences

Analysis of Leitana Nehan's partnership with both IWDA and AusAID does reflect this description. While these organisations do share a common vision and collaborate quite frequently on a number of fronts, the fundamental issue that underpins their relationship is funding. In other words, their partnership is by no means influenced by policy dialogue alone.

While Leitana Nehan has benefited from this model of partnership by successfully implementing its programs, its success stories are, to a larger extent, dependent on how the organisation has managed to negotiate the 'conditionalities' and/or strings attached to the aid package (see Stokke 1995; Sogge 2002). INTRAC (2001:4) observes that 'the control-orientation of funding systems is thought to be somewhat excessive even among the NGO staff themselves'. Donor agencies' indirect power and implicit influence can exert substantial pressure on recipient NGOs, ultimately reducing them to being mere followers rather than having the leverage to share the aid governance. My experience in conducting research in this field reveals that NGOs rarely criticise donors' neoliberal agendas for fear of losing funding, particularly when the recipient NGOs are completely donor-dependent. For example, in one attempt to discuss funding issues with one of the three organisations, the officers concerned with the issues showed little interest in engaging in the discussion (Makuwira 2003). While this may be as a result of other genuine reasons, it does illustrate the dilemma inherent in the whole debate of aid and partnerships.

Capacity-based differences

What triggers many emerging NGOs to seek funding from the donor community is the fact that the NGOs themselves lack both strong human and material resource bases. Emerging NGOs in conflict and post-conflict situations can hardly be described as resource-rich. Leitana Nehan started out with relatively low-level capacity to undertake programs, compared to its international partners. Leitana Nehan's partnerships with donor agencies was mainly founded on financial need, since they had plenty of volunteers to fill their human resource requirements at the local level. However, the combination of outside financial support and local human resource support has resulted in a substantial increase in the organisation's capacity to develop, deliver and evaluate projects, thus overcoming some of the capacity-based differences between Leitana Nehan and its partners.

Trust-based differences

Trust is one of the fundamental pillars of aid partnership, although there are often disparities in practice. Leitana Nehan's partnerships with IWDA, AusAID, NZAID and Oxfam New Zealand are positioned at various points along the trust continuum. In a way, these partnerships can neither be described as 'total control' nor 'unconditional trust'. Accountability and transparency have become the barometer through which NGOs engaged in any form of aid partnership have to demonstrate their ability to comply with the 'standard' required by donors. Because donors hold an upper hand in terms of dictating the modalities of aid management, recipient NGOs are usually required to comply and demonstrate this compliance by being highly accountable to the donors rather than to the NGOs' own constituencies. Leitana Nehan's modest start, managing small amounts of funds responsibly and accountably and submitting project reports diligently, seems to have won the trust of many donor agencies, particularly IWDA.

LEITANA NEHAN AND BOUGAINVILLE PROVINCIAL GOVERNMENT PARTNERSHIP

Quite a number of cases demonstrate Leitana Nehan's collaborative partnerships with the various forms of the Bougainville Provincial Government. Over the past few years Leitana Nehan has actively participated in a number of constitutional review processes leading up to the election of the Autonomous Bougainville Government (ABG), and has frequently been involved in meetings and fora with some government departments.

The partnership model Leitana Nehan has adopted in its relationship with the government is predominantly a third-sector dominant model. As an autonomous organisation, Leitana Nehan seeks funding, identifies programs, implements, monitors and evaluates them virtually independently of government, although officers from some government departments may become involved to some degree as observers or workshop participants. Leitana Nehan also engages in a dual model of NGO–government partnership, largely because the current government does not have the capacity to provide services to every sector of development. As such, many NGOs in Bougainville, including Leitana Nehan, are 'gap-fillers'.

Precisely because governments and NGOs are organised differently and use contrasting approaches to development and peace-building issues, they are likely, at times, to come into conflict. In a region as diverse as the Pacific islands, government–NGO relations may vary with place and time. To begin with, the government has to establish trust with civil society organisations. This is not an easy thing to do, particularly an emerging NGO sector which may have different values and agendas to the government.

There is also an emerging trend in many countries now to formulate codes of conduct (Bennett 1997), which helps both NGOs and government to adhere to a particular standard of operation. Although this is a controversial issue among NGOs, who view this as limiting their freedom, it does have the potential to facilitate government–

NGO partnerships. Smillie (1995:74) takes the issue further and recommends that

> Government can influence the climate for NGOs in a variety of formal and informal ways. On the informal side, government can foster what has become known as 'enabling environment' collaboration, consultation, assistance in coordination, and by sending positive messages to the media and to the public that NGOs have a beneficial and welcome role to play in development.

In the lead up to autonomy, and in the time since, communication and the sharing of information and ideas between NGOs and the provincial government have increased (see Epilogue).

LEITANA NEHAN AND OTHER NGO PARTNERSHIPS

Leitana Nehan's partnerships with other NGOs in Bougainville and in the Pacific islands have been well documented in earlier chapters, and also to a lesser extent in Böge and Garasu (2004). Leitana Nehan networks locally with a range of NGOs, including the Bougainville Interchurch Women's Forum, Peace Foundation Melanesia, Bougainville Trauma Institute, Bougainville Catholic Family Life, Bougainville Provincial Council of Women, and the Bougainville Provincial AIDS Council. These organisations share skills and resources as well as information. Leitana Nehan is a key NGO in these partnerships (Böge and Garasu 2004). Furthermore, one of Leitana Nehan's board members is also on the board of BICWF, while Agnes Titus is on the board of Bougainville Microfinance and the Bougainville Provincial AIDS Council.

With regards to the international NGOs operating in Bougainville, Leitana Nehan's staff have also served as members on some of their boards (personal comm., Helen Hakena, 30 September 2004). Internationally, Leitana Nehan is a member of many networks, such as International Action Network Against Small Arms, the Pacific Women Against Violence Network, the Women and Peace Building Network, World Vision, Callan Services, UNICEF, UNDP, and UNAids. These networks assist in advocacy, lobbying for policy changes and training. As noted in previous chapters, there has been substantial collaboration with the Fiji Women's Crisis Centre and, to a lesser extent, the Asian and Pacific Development Centre, based in Malaysia. The Asian and Pacific Development Centre, 'through its publication and seminar programs, offered Leitana Nehan valuable opportunities to express itself and learn from relevant comparative experiences' (Carl 2000:13).

LEITANA NEHAN AND ITS LOCAL COMMUNITY MEMBERS

Leitana Nehan's success stories lie in their strategic direction, which are grounded in the practical applications of participatory development and empowerment discourse. It has organised and implemented numerous workshops using participatory approaches that encouraged participants to contribute to decision-making processes (see Chapters 3–5). Cox (2004a) documents the increasing number of people volunteering to facilitate Leitana Nehan's work, which demonstrates the working partnerships between the organisation and the broader community. According to Hakena (2003a), this spirit lies in the feeling of a sense of ownership.

WHAT LESSONS HAVE WE LEARNT?

Leitana Nehan's partnerships with other stakeholders, including its beneficiaries, illustrate the complexity of aid and aid agencies in post-conflict peace-building and development. To begin this analysis it is vital to reflect on the sentiments of Ahai who contends that

> donor countries, as well as international NGOs, will need to be sensitive to the development aspirations of Bougainvilleans, even within the political framework of PNG, and design the delivery of their support in ways that are mutually beneficial. The current practice in a few international NGOs...of bringing in outsiders will simply promote the 'cargo development mentality' typical of pre-crisis development (1999:135).

Bougainville in crisis needed outside support from partner organisations capable of understanding the conflict's causes and history. The story of Leitana Nehan, as with other local organisations in Bougainville, is of passion and determination to initiate change amid internal tensions. It motivates the readers to reflect on what can be done when conflicts divide once-cohesive communities. Beyond this, the story challenges the simplistic view that aid is a means to an end.

More importantly, it elucidates that building partnerships for post-conflict peace-building and development is no smooth undertaking.

Partnership-building, as shown by this case, starts with an honest feeling and acceptance that something somewhere is not right. The media's contribution to making some of the conflicts known to the outside world varies in degree and accuracy, but when such conflicts are reported by insiders, the truthfulness of their reports can have a profound impact on the audience. For Leitana Nehan, revealing the conflict's effects on Bougainville women not only opened opportunities for collaboration with other organisations but also marked the beginning of funding and institutional capacity-building. Over time, Leitana Nehan's capacity to engage in a multi-partnership collaboration increased substantially. What is critical in Leitana Nehan's partnerships is its willingness to engage in such dialogue and partnering on the basis of shared vision and/or commonality of purpose.

As has been noted in the literature, the politics of aid raises a number of questions, especially with regard to its effectiveness, based on the modalities of donor coordination, the question of ownership, to whom recipient organisations should be accountable, and the dynamics of transparency in both donor and recipient countries (Stokke 1995; UNESCO 2000). Leitana Nehan's partnership with IWDA is, to a certain degree, a classic example of how two organisations with fundamentally similar vision and values enter into partnership. The case demonstrates that, where external factors and/or influences are kept constant, the potential for positive impact is very high. However, two issues need to be made explicit. While such partnerships may be driven by an organisation's missions and objectives, the donor agencies need to understand the sensitivities of post-conflict dynamics. The fundamental issue is ensuring that a partnership does not become part of the problem or exacerbate the problem. As an intermediary NGO, IWDA may be influenced by its funders' visions of how things should be done. Tensions can break out when beneficiaries' expecations differ wildly from those of the funding agency. In the case of Leitana Nehan and IWDA/AusAID, such contradictions have been minimal, largely because of Leitana Nehan's experience with international aid agencies and understanding of donor conditionalities.

Leitana Nehan's collaboration with other NGOs, as presented in this case study, equally offers some interesting parallels with the wider literature on inter-NGO relationships. While there are indications of good working relationships between and among NGOs in Bougainville, there is very little evidence, even within the wider literature in post-conflict situations, of what impact this collaboration has had, whether collaboration has been informal or formal, or whether partnerships go beyond mere consultation.

Similarly, Leitana Nehan's partnership with the government and its beneficiaries has raised many questions. Given the enormous developmental challenges of post-conflict areas, it is ideal that the government take the lead in crafting a post-conflict reconstruction plan. While evidence suggests that Leitana Nehan continues to contribute to development and peace-building activities in Bougainville, the fact that many of its activities are dictated by donor agencies' funding and influence raises questions about the impact of these on the organisation's relationship with the interim government. Further research could be done to ascertain the government's views on the role of NGOs and civil society organisations in peace-building and development in Bougainville. Furthermore, there is very little information on how the current interim government provides a conducive environment for NGOs like Leitana Nehan to maximise the results of their peace-building activities.

As noted earlier, Leitana Nehan's role in peace-building and development is seen by the extent to which beneficiaries are engaged in the decision-making processes that affect them. While evidence suggests that this has been accomplished through various consultative meetings and workshops in Leitana Nehan's constituencies, corroborating this claim is a challenging undertaking in post-conflict situations, as not many people will speak freely. Overall, what this case has done is to provide some snapshots of the kinds of partnerships that can be developed. In addition, it also provides an indicator of the difficulties that NGOs encounter when donor agencies use intermediary organisations as conduits for channelling funds to recipient organisations.

CONCLUSION

The analysis in this chapter attempts to provide grounds for further debate and reflection. Leitana Nehan's work concurs with Patrick (2000:37), who believes that 'to be effective, reconstruction assistance must be prompt, coherent and responsive to local needs'. Leitana Nehan has shown a very clear understanding of local social, cultural and political dynamics, and this has enhanced its partnership-building efforts. Whether on not donor agencies design the conditions to advance peace, however, is a question that needs further examination. Perhaps further reflection is required on the question of 'interest', in light of long-term benefits, not from the perspective of donors but the intended beneficiaries. From a social justice perspective, any partnership in which a large outside donor focuses on self-interest is in danger of proceeding at the expense of the poor, displaced or marginalised, should be called into question. Leitana Nehan, however, has for the most part averted this danger by partnering with international NGOs who share the same visions, are willing to collaborate as equals, can provide suitable levels of resources, and with whom they can develop relationships of trust.

NOTE

[1]   We are using the terms 'North' to denote countries in the developed world, and 'South', to denote countries in the developing world.

8 NON-GOVERNMENT ORGANISATIONS, PEACE-BUILDING AND GLOBAL NETWORKS

Peter Ninnes

In the first section of this book we described and explained the work of Leitana Nehan from its inception in 1992 until the end of the 'Strengthening Communities for Peace' project. I showed how it began with somewhat *ad hoc* work with women, focusing on humanitarian relief and awareness-raising tasks during the crisis. To this was added peace-building work, particularly in the form of 'mobilisations' of women and youth. These large meetings were supported by small grants from local and international organisations. As well as their impact on the participants, they provided Leitana Nehan with a range of organisational, fund-raising and networking experiences and contributed to the development of a cadre of volunteers to assist the founders and their spouses. The formal end of the crisis provided new opportunities for organisational learning, through attending conferences and meetings, undertaking training, and meeting with supporters and partners. In recent years, the organisation has extended its work with significant grants in partnership with overseas NGOs and government development agencies. The majority of this work has involved awareness-raising, advocacy, community development training and counselling, with a focus on women's and children's rights, prevention of violence against women, and alcohol abuse.

In the second section of the book, I have analysed the work of Leitana Nehan through a number of lenses. In Chapter 6, I explored the uses and origins of a range of discourses of gender, development and peace employed by Leitana Nehan. I argued that discourses are productive, because they both limit and expand the way we see ourselves and our relationships to other people and to the world. Leitana Nehan has both been exposed to, and deployed, a variety of discourses that have helped them and the participants in their programs reimagine gender relations, development and peace in Bougainville. In Chapter 7, Jonathan Makuwira described and analysed the major partnerships in which Leitana Nehan has been involved, and teased out some of the common interests that sustained those partnerships, as well the tensions that are inherent in them.

The purpose of this chapter is to analyse Leitana Nehan's work in terms of three broader sets of ideas. First I reflect on the organisation's work in the light of the literature about effective non-government organisations. I first review this literature, and then examine the extent to which Leitana Nehan's longevity and success can be attributed to the way it operates as an NGO, the effective practices it has employed, any new insights about NGO operation that Leitana Nehan reveals, and any differences between the literature and Leitana Nehan's operations that might constitute a threat to Leitana Nehan's continued work.

Second, I reflect on Leitana Nehan's work in the light of the literature on peace-building. After a brief review of relevant literature, I analyse the extent to which Leitana Nehan has conformed to the practices and approaches found to be successful elsewhere. I explore if there are any gaps in the Leitana Nehan approach, or any new insights or lessons that can be learned for peace-building work in general.

Third, and drawing on elements of the NGO and peace-building literature, I map the relationships and networks that Leitana Nehan has developed over time, as means of explaining the complexity and characteristics of the networks that have been required to undertake successful peace-building work in conflict and post-conflict contexts.

EFFECTIVE NGOS

Non-government organisations comprise a complex and multi-faceted part of civil society. In the past, they have been classified geographically as local, national and international, functionally as operational (providing programs) and advocacy NGOs, and in terms of their focus on human rights or development (van Tuijl 1999; Scott 2001). However, as van Tuijl (1999) observes, these distinctions are becoming blurred as NGOs recognise the links between human rights and development (see also Angeles 2003), the need to advocate for policies that support programs (see also Fitzduff and Church 2004), and as they become enmeshed in denser transnational networks. Edwards (1999) contrasts the effectiveness of development agencies on the one hand and social movements such as the environmental movement and the women's movement on the other hand. Yet many NGOs work within 'development' while being part of social movements (see, for example, Chen Jie 2001). In addition, some NGOs are becoming quasi-government organisations as they receive funding from governments and provide social services previously provided by the state (Hilhorst 2003; van Tuijl 1999)

The effectiveness of NGOs can be constrained by a number of factors outside their organisations. For example, Ewig (1999), analysing the situation in Nicaragua, observes that NGO success depended in part on the presence of elected or non-elected government officials who were sympathetic to NGOs' goals, as well as a government policy framework that allowed NGOs both to exist and flourish. In Sudan, Yongo-Bure (2003) observed that a lack of basic infrastructure —such as roads—prevented NGO programs being effectively implemented. Chen Jie (2001) argues that in Taiwan, a lack of formal diplomatic recognition has constrained the extent to which local NGOS can form links with outside organisations. Diminishing levels of official development assistance are also likely to impact on NGO operations, although some authors believe this represents an opportunity for northern and southern NGOs to transform their relationships from dependency to more substantive partnerships (Malhotra 2000) or for NGOs to embrace human rights rather than development as their dominant focus (van Tuijl 2000).

Even in contexts where policy, personnel, infrastructure and international relations issues enhance or support NGO operations, there are a number of approaches concerning the actual ways in which development NGOs operate that can be effective. Edwards (1999) suggests a range of effective approaches. Although his remarks are made in the context of development projects undertaken primarily by large-scale NGOs, they may well apply to a wider range of NGO operations. According to Edwards, factors contributing to the success of development projects include meeting local needs and assuming that local people have the competence to deal with these needs; ensuring beneficiaries participate at every stage; taking into account local cultural and political issues rather than simply viewing the project in terms of technical problems to be solved; finding the right mix between local and imported knowledge, while ensuring local control of the process; reducing dependency and increasing autonomy; finding a balance between material, social and institutional development; and organising in groups and linking groups together.

Edwards (1999) also emphasises three generic practices. First, local capacity needs to be strengthened so that people can identify problems and solutions and develop wide-ranging support for proposed actions. Second, outputs need to be produced which are valued by a large proportion of the population and opposed by only a few, and this depends on developing strong links between various sectors of the community. Third, 'help' needs to be in the right form. In particular, it needs to ensure local ownership and provide time and space to learn lessons and develop capacity and linkages.

LEITANA NEHAN AS AN NGO

In analysing Leitana Nehan's work, we now turn to a discussion of the extent to which Leitana Nehan has used the approaches and practices advocated by Edwards (1999). These approaches and practices were advocated in the context of development projects. Therefore, they may be more relevant to the various projects in which Leitana Nehan has engaged, from the women's and youth mobilisations to the SCP. They may be less relevant to other work Leitana Nehan has done, such as counselling, advocacy and the radio program.

　　1. *Meeting local needs and assuming that local people have the competence to deal with these needs.* The preceding chapters indicate that Leitana Nehan has responded to a wide range of local needs. During the crisis, Leitana Nehan initially met the needs of

women and children in care centres, particularly in terms of supplying them with second-hand clothes. They also met the needs of people in other parts of Bougainville, by organising for medicines to be smuggled across the blockade. Through their mobilisations, they also met the need for people to begin to learn from and develop trust in each other, to deal with the effects of the crisis, and to begin to imagine a new way of living together. Leitana Nehan's awareness workshops have met a need to find ways to reduce violence in communities, while their counselling services have met the need for trauma counselling. The second phase of the Strengthening Communities for Peace project also began to meet the socioeconomic development needs of communities. Leitana Nehan recognised that, once communities had dealt with issues such as alcohol abuse and violence, they needed to find constructive activities for community members. SCP 2 therefore included a process of community development training and capacity-building for raising funds to meet local economic development needs. Although Edwards (1999) argues that effective NGOs need to meet local needs, Leitana Nehan shows that effective NGOs in the long term identify and respond to changing needs resulting from changing political, economic and social circumstances. The SCP project also shows the way in which Leitana Nehan has expected communities to have the competence to deal with their own issues. While Leitana Nehan provided ideas about how to conceptualise issues affecting communities, the teams working in villages and schools left it up to those communities to decide on their own solutions. There were also occasions, however, when people were not able to help themselves. In Bougainville, this was often because people were afraid or were traumatised by the war. Effective NGOs in post-conflict situations, therefore, should not only meet local needs, but also carefully assess the extent to which the conflict has impacted people's competence, that is, their ability to act. Another problem in Edwards' (1999) local-needs approach revealed by Leitana Nehan's work is that Edwards appears to assume that needs are out there in the community and the NGO has to identify them somehow. In Leitana Nehan's case, however, there is a much more dynamic relationship between the organisation, the community and needs, which disrupts Edwards' binary of 'communities with needs' and 'NGOs discovering needs'. First, the paid and volunteer workers in Leitana Nehan are all members of Bougainville communities. In the SCP, the members of district teams were all members of communities in those districts. Thus, to some extent, the needs of the communities were the needs of the Leitana Nehan workers. Second, communities have problems which they can identify, but what they 'need' to deal with those problems is negotiated and constructed through a variety of mechanisms, including the introduction of new ideas into communities through Leitana Nehan's workshops and the radio program.

2. *Ensuring beneficiaries participate at every stage.* As noted above, since Leitana Nehan workers are members of Bougainville communities, they are also beneficiaries of Leitana Nehan's programs. In addition, all of the small and large projects in which Leitana Nehan has been involved have been highly participatory. The women's and youth mobilisations were not just passive occasions in which audience members listened to speakers. Rather, they were times of sharing, singing, praying, creating, and witnessing. The awareness workshops, both before and during the SCP project, were also highly participatory. The workshops were open to all members of the community. At the same time, Edwards' (1999) idea is challenged by Leitana Nehan's post-conflict anti-violence work because the workshops were not only open to beneficiaries, such as women who would benefit from less violence, and community members who would benefit from reduced alcohol abuse, they were also open to members of the community who may have perpetrated violence or who had patriarchal ideas about gender relations.

3. *Taking into account local cultural and political issues rather than simply viewing the project in terms of technical problems to be solved.* It is notable that the members of Leitana Nehan have

almost never conceptualised their work in terms of a technical problem to be solved. Indeed, one way of positioning Leitana Nehan's work is at the cutting edge of cultural, social and political change. As we saw in Chapter 6, the focus of their work is at the point where indigenous cultural practices and politics intersect with local, regional and global cultural practices and politics in the form of the church, international human rights norms and conventions, and national and provincial constitutions and laws. Therefore, Leitana Nehan's effectiveness can be attributed not just to a 'taking into account' of local culture and politics, but a dynamic, complex, informed, and committed engagement in the cultural politics of gender, development and peace in Bougainville.

4. *Finding the right mix between local and imported knowledge, while ensuring local control of the process.* Leitana Nehan has used a mix of local and imported knowledge. However, their work involves more than simply 'finding the right mix'; it involves actively engaging in a wide range of discussions at community and provincial levels about the composition of that mix. As a local NGO with competent and well-connected leaders, Leitana Nehan has for the most part maintained control of the process. At times, they have gratefully accepted advice from outside consultants, while ignoring other suggestions. The Leitana Nehan constitution, for example, reads in places like a template from overseas, but there are some clauses such as those to do with membership for women only, that they have not instigated. On the other hand, the SCP project at times stretched Leitana Nehan's ability to control the process. In particular, AusAID's demands that teams be implemented in all districts within a certain timeframe was not Leitana Nehan's preferred mode of operating, but needed to be followed as AusAID was funding the program.

5. *Reducing dependency and increasing autonomy.* In terms of human resource development, Leitana Nehan has been very effective in reducing dependence on outside expertise and developing

their ability to run the organisation autonomously. In particular, through their years of experience, they have become adept at writing applications, reporting on project progress, and acquitting donor funds. Furthermore, they have become skilled in managing Leitana Nehan. The contribution of the late George Lesi was very important. He brought to Leitana Nehan his training and long experience in organisational management, which helped Leitana Nehan clarify workers' roles and reporting lines. On the other hand, Leitana Nehan has not been able to develop a substantial independent revenue stream. That is, their major work continues to rely on overseas funds. The SCP was funded by AusAID for four years, but once the project was complete, the workshops and other activities ceased, except in a few cases where members of volunteer teams ran occasional workshops in their home districts on a *pro bono* basis. Yet the SCP only covered a handful of the communities in each district, and many more communities could benefit from similar programs. In late 2004, Leitana Nehan received a new major grant from NZ Aid. However, this funding was mainly for counselling programs in the thirteen districts. Thus, while the work of Leitana Nehan continued, the scope and thrust of the work has been dictated to a large extent by what outside donors are willing to fund. These problems of project-based work are well known in the wider development community (Edwards 1999).

6. *Finding a balance between material, social and institutional development.* Much of Leitana Nehan's work has been conceptualised as involving psychological and spiritual development as a precursor to social and economic development. It is worth noting that in a later paper, Edwards and Sen (2000) argue that NGOs have not focused enough on changing people's hearts. Leitana Nehan, however, has taken personal change as the starting point for social and institutional change. At the same time, Leitana Nehan has not ignored those other aspects. The SPC began to deal with issues of socioeconomic development. In recent years, Leitana Nehan

has also conducted gender awareness for police, the judiciary, nurses and teachers, thus contributing to institutional change in such areas as the treatment of rape victims in hospitals, the methods of police investigation of rape and domestic assault, and the conduct of sexual assault trials.

7. *Organising in groups and linking groups together.* The use of groups of various sizes and compositions has been one of the hallmarks of Leitana Nehan's work. In the beginning, Leitana Nehan was founded by a group of four friends. Although Helen had been doing some advocacy work on her own, this work began to expand once her three former school friends joined her. This original group was supported by another group of resource people that included several of their spouses. The initial mobilisations provided opportunities to articulate Leitana Nehan's ideals and purposes and to identify and recruit further volunteers. In the SCP, the team-based approach meant that Leitana Nehan's work could be spread into all districts of Bougainville. These teams were linked in two ways. First, the organisation provided project officers who had oversight of a number of teams. Second, the teams gathered together for training and program review at various times, which provided opportunities for interaction between members of different teams.

8. *Strengthening local capacity.* Leitana Nehan has contributed to strengthening local capacity at a number of levels. First, the founding members and their support group have expanded their skills in a wide range of areas, including management, advocacy, counselling and training of trainers. Second, more than 90 volunteers have been trained in gender awareness, violence prevention, presentation skills and workshop planning and evaluation, and many volunteer counsellors have been trained. Third, the teams themselves have trained people in the villages in terms of gender awareness, violence against women, alcohol abuse, and to undertake community mapping, identify their needs, and source funds to undertake programs of importance to them. In Leitana Nehan's case, the capacity that has been strengthened is not just in terms of technical

skills. Rather, Leitana Nehan's work has enhanced people's awareness of, and ability to conceptualise and address issues pertaining to gender, violence, rights and a range of other relevant social problems. In other words, it has been a process of both raising awareness and building capacity.

9. *Producing valued outputs and developing strong links between various sectors of the community.* There are many pieces of evidence that the work undertaken by Leitana Nehan is valued by various sectors in the community, and only a few examples are mentioned here. First, one long-standing volunteer reported that the personality integration workshops were a 'hit' with young people because they improved their self-esteem. Second, some of the team members reported that requests for involvement in SCP came after community members heard the Leitana Nehan radio program. Third, in some places, community members have asked for further workshops after the SCP program was completed. Fourth, people often saw the results of Leitana Nehan's work in other communities, such as the reduction in homebrew production and consumption, and wanted similar changes for themselves. At the same time, some team members reported resistance to their work. In one of the patrilineal communities in Bougainville, the team leader reported that men in the community had accused the Leitana Nehan team of trying to change custom when they spoke out against wife-beating. The same men also were offended by female team members 'telling men what to do'. Another team, working in one of the districts near the former copper mine, were met with suspicion in two communities. The team leader believed that the communities thought that Leitana Nehan had a hidden agenda of getting the mine operational again.

10. *'Help' is provided and received that ensures local ownership and provides time and space to learn lessons and develop capacity and linkages.* The 'help' that Leitana Nehan has received from outside organisations has for the most part ensured that Leitana Nehan has had substantial control and ownership of their programs. In the early days, the small grants of several thousand

kina for organising mobilisations came with few strings attached. Leitana Nehan was free to organise the meetings in ways that they believed would be effective. Later large grants, such as the two phases of the SCP, had more strings attached in terms of reporting requirements and the timeframe in which the projects had to be completed. On the other hand, major components of the SCP projects were based on activities and strategies that Leitana Nehan had used in the past, and which were deemed to be suitable to the needs and contexts of Bougainville communities. It should also be noted that these major projects were only funded after Leitana Nehan had spent eight years learning lessons and developing its capacity and links to outside organisations. In this regard, Leitana Nehan provides a close fit with this aspect of Edwards' (1999) theory of effective NGO practices. The characteristics and extent of the linkages that Leitana Nehan has developed are discussed in more detail in the final section of this chapter.

EFFECTIVE PEACE-BUILDING

Whereas peace-making is the process of bringing armed conflict to an end, peace-building involves creating a set of conditions where people are not inclined to resort to violence as a means of solving their problems (Brand-Jacobsen and Jacobsen 2000). Lederach (1997) identifies three major tasks of peace-building in post-conflict recovery, namely, rebuilding infrastructure, re-establishing social institutions, and reconciliation. Although Lederach's scenario is an ideal-type, Rigby (2001) identifies purposefully forgetting, pursuing justice, truth-telling, and compensation and reparation as alternative or additional processes to reconciliation. Spence (1999) notes the need for social, political and economic reconstruction, and the repatriation and demobilisation of combatants. Harris (1999) adds a further task—the construction of a new, peaceful vision for society. This vision of society needs to address the underlying causes of the conflict, which are often grounded in inequity, poverty, or other forms of structural violence (Harris and Lewis 1999a; see also Rigby 2001; Junne and Verkoren 2005). Furthermore, armed conflict is traumatic, and part of the reconciliation process involves dealing with a wide range of psychological issues that arise (Lewis 1999a).

In terms of NGOs' role in peace-building, Harris and Lewis (1999b) argue that, although many international NGOs play prominent roles in post-conflict recovery, these are not unproblematic. International NGOs can be flexible, responsive and able to work with local partners, while advocating for marginalised groups. Many, however, run programs without accountability and evaluation, are linked to government aid agencies in their home countries, compete with each other for funds, and fail to coordinate efforts with other organisations. Furthermore, they often represent the local people as helpless and childlike. International NGOs traditionally focus on reconstruction, but they can also contribute in human rights work, trauma recovery, conflict resolution, policy advocacy and so on, as well as helping local NGOs develop and strengthen their capacities (Harris and Lewis 1999b). Spence (1999) adds that International NGOs and local NGOs need to use local knowledge, avoid top-down approaches, use participatory approaches, and act as advocates against injustice. Of relevance here, Lewis (1999b) notes the importance of dealing with sexual assault issues as part of post-conflict reconstruction and the dangers of using culturally sensitive approaches to gender relations that often reproduce patriarchal relations and, by limiting the involvement of women, reduce the extent to which human resources for peace and development are established.

Reviewing two decades of peace-building work in a wide range of countries and contexts, Lederach (2005) has identified four practices that he argues comprise the components of a 'moral imagination' and that are essential for peace-building work. The first of these is relationships. Peace-building, Lederach argues, 'must experience, envision and give birth to the [new] web of relationships' (2005:34). This involves developing relationships, networking, and acknowledging interdependence and mutuality. These new webs require humility and self-recognition: the builders of the webs need to see themselves as part of the previous, destructive pattern and take responsibility for changing it.

Second, peace-builders need to have and nurture 'paradoxical curiosity' (Lederach 2005:35). Many conflicts are conceptualised in terms of 'us and them' dualisms. The moral imagination refuses simplistic binaries or polarities. Lederach uses 'paradox' here in the sense of that which is outside that normally considered to be true. By curiosity, Lederach (2005) means careful inquiry that goes beyond established meanings. Paradoxical curiosity then 'approaches social realities with an abiding respect for complexity, a refusal to fall prey to the pressures of forced dualistic categories of truth, and an inquisitiveness about what may hold together seemingly contradictory social energies in a greater whole' (2005:36). On the one hand paradoxical curiosity takes people and their experiences at face value; on the other hand it explores the deeper meanings of what people value and their experiences. It suspends value judgements. It views complexity as a friend out of which new possibilities will become apparent (2005).

Third, peace builders need to employ creativity that 'moves beyond what exists toward something new and unexpected while rising from and speaking to the everyday' (Lederach 2005:38). Furthermore, in the peace-building process, space needs to be provided for creative acts to occur. Lederach also adds that peace-building can include input from groups in the community whose work involves creativity, such as artists.

Finally, peace-builders need to be willing to take risks (Lederach 2005). These risks have no guarantee of safety or success. In violent conflict, peace is a mystery and therefore it takes a risk to move in the direction of peace. According to Lederach (2005:163), 'risk accepts vulnerability and lets go of the need to *a priori* control the process or the outcomes of human affairs'. Risk in peace-building particularly involves seeking 'constructive engagement with those people and things we least understand and most fear' (2005:173).

LEITANA NEHAN AS PEACE-BUILDER

Leitana Nehan has contributed to many tasks indentified above as peace-building; in particular, it has contributed to providing a new vision for peace, psychological recovery, reconciliation, the re-establishment and.re-thinking of social institutions, especially families and villages, but also political institutions, through its advocacy for women's and children's rights to be recognised at the provincial level. As a local NGO, Leitana Nehan has avoided many of the pitfalls encountered by international NGOs undertaking peace-building work. In this section of the chapter, however, I want to explore Leitana Nehan's work through the lens of Lederach's four principles of peace-building and discuss the extent to which Leitana Nehan's effectiveness as a peace-builder can be explained in terms of those four principles.

1. *Developing relationships and networks across boundaries, taking responsibility and acknowledging mutuality.* The extent and characteristics of the relationships and networks that Leitana Nehan has developed are explored in detail in the last section of this chapter. Here it is important to make a number of points. First, as a local NGO, Leitana Nehan at its founding already had a wide set of relationships and networks in place. As noted in earlier chapters, Leitana Nehan's founders had a range of affiliations in the Provincial Council of Women, in the Catholic Women's Association, in the chiefly social system, among their school alumni and so on. They also had networks resulting from their pre-crisis employment as teachers, welfare workers and accountants. Furthermore, their support group also had contacts, such as through the local business community. During the crisis, and in the post-conflict period, Leitana Nehan has developed a wide range of contacts in the local, national and international NGO community, among politicians, civil servants, and with other denominations. The relationships that they have built across gender and political boundaries are of major importance to their peace building efforts. The fact that they have included both men and women in their teams has indicated their willingness to make gender equity a community-wide issue and effort. The fact that they have included ex-combatants from all sides of the conflict, as well as people from communities who did not take sides, indicates their willingness to establish relationships across previously impenetrable barriers. Boundary crossing was also exhibited in

the inclusive nature of the large youth mobilisations held in the late 1990s (see Chapter 3), which brought together youth from all the major Christian denominations in Bougainville. Some boundaries have been more difficult to cross than others. From time to time there are tensions between NGOs on Bougainville, and some of these fractures occur along lines created during the conflict. Leitana Nehan has also been prominent in its willingness to take responsibility for peace-building. One of the rationales for the founding of Leitana Nehan was the realisation that 'we must help ourselves' (Chapter 2). Furthermore, their training and deployment of ex-combatants as volunteers provides opportunities for these groups to take responsibility for building peace. The Leitana Nehan founders also acknowledge mutuality. As noted in Chapter 6, Leitana Nehan workers and founders often conceptualise peace as a process that begins through an acknowledgement of one's own need to change.

2. *Exhibiting and practising paradoxical curiosity, including a refusal to employ binaries, breaking out of the mould and entertaining paradoxes.* Leitana Nehan displays these attributes in a number of ways. For example, the ways in which Leitana Nehan conceptualises gender, explored in Chapter 6, represent a complex constellation of liberal, cultural and radical cultural ideas which, it might be argued, are mutually exclusive but which Leitana Nehan employs simultaneously. This approach allows them to reject binaries which view women's and men's interests as diametrically opposed, and instead provides a context in which unique contributions are celebrated and affirmed while recognising the need for all community members to contribute to gender work. The wide extent of Leitana Nehan's networks, discussed below, indicates the willingness of the Leitana Nehan leaders to take at face value people who are willing to contribute to their work. At the same time, Leitana Nehan does not necessarily subscribe to an identical set of values with all the people with whom they work and collaborate. Their engagement with the Catholic church is a prime example. The church and Leitana Nehan have many values in common, but certain aspects

of women's rights, for example, are problematic. Nevertheless, Leitana Nehan leaders are able to accommodate and work with complex relationships such as these.

3. *Creatively going beyond the normal order of things.* Many aspects of Leitana Nehan's work reflect a creative approach to building peace in Bougainville that goes beyond the normal order of things. Leitana Nehan employs both men and women to address issues of gender; it employs both ex-combatants and non-combatants to address issues of non-violence; and it employs former producers and consumers of homebrew to educate people about the dangers of alcohol. The leaders of Leitana Nehan have also been creative in the way they have been able to seize opportunities as they arise. The visit by a Save the Children representative, described in Chapter 2, was seized as a way of (creatively) distributing medicines in Bougainville. The suspension of regulations limiting public gatherings in 1994 was seized as an opportunity to mobilise women for peace and hold the Bougainville Reunion at Hahela. Smuggling the video of that event out of the country was also a creative act. Employing a man, the late George Lesi, as deputy executive director of a women's agency may also seem beyond the normal order of things, but he brought a commitment to the issues and crucial managerial skills to the organisation. The Silent March in Buka (see Chapter 3) was creatively timed to coincide with a visit to Buka by the prime minister of Papua New Guinea and the accompanying media contingent. The use of deliberately vague statements about the goals of the November 1997 youth mobilisation (see Chapter 3) was also a creative act. In addition to creative thinking and strategising, Leitana Nehan has sometimes used creative methods in its programs; the Hihatuts Theatre Troupe (see Chapter 4) is an excellent example. Other examples include the use of story, song, and poetry-writing in youth mobilisations (Chapter 3), and the use of locally created visual aids such as posters in awareness workshops.

4. *Taking risks.* Letian Nehan's work, described in the previous chapters, demonstrates Lederach's (2005) idea that effective peace-

building involves taking risks. In the case of Leitana Nehan, these risks have taken a number of forms. First, moving back to Buka in late 1990 after the return of the PNGDF represented a risk given the armed forces' lack of discipline. Advising women about safety issues was also risky. Distributing clothes and medicines to people around Bougainville was risky, as was holding the Silent March in 1995. Delivering clothes to Sam Kauona in the bush and flying in to meet women behind the blockade were also risky endeavours. Even travelling to Port Moresby, as most Leitana Nehan workers and volunteers need to do in order to travel overseas or to other parts of Papua New Guinea, was risky, as Helen discovered when she was threatened at the airport there (see Chapter 3). Previous chapters described many other examples of Leitana Nehan staff risking physical harm to carry out their work. In addition to physical harm, Leitana Nehan has been willing to take risks in terms of both its initial establishment and its subsequent development of contacts and supporters. For example, the initial break with the Provincial Council of Women in 1995 risked alienating potential allies and represented a major move into the unknown. Becoming an organisation that worked with a wide array of groups locally, nationally and internationally, including in the case of Leitana Nehan, men, ex-combatants, academics, consultants, project managers and so on is also risky, because such groups and individuals may not understand or entirely share the values and goals of the organisation. Furthermore, there is a risk that the greater access to funds or ideas may allow outside groups to exert undue control over the organisation's direction. In Lederach's (2005) terms, Leitana Nehan and its leaders have in fact been willing to take risks that expose their vulnerability and that present the possibility of not being able to control proceedings completely. In addition, they have constructively engaged with actors or members of groups that have not always acted in the best interests of women or Bougainvilleans in other contexts. Such inclusive, risky and paradoxical approaches are a major reason for Leitana Nehan's success as a peace-building organisation.

THE NETWORKED NGO

One common focus in the literature on effective NGOs and effective peace-building reviewed is the importance of creating linkages, relationships and networks. In the case of Leitana Nehan, Jonathan Makuwira explored one aspect of Leitana Nehan's network in the previous chapter by examining its partnership with IWDA and AusAID. But, like many effective local NGOs, Leitana Nehan is part of a wider network, and a component of a worldwide transnational advocacy movement concerned with the promotion of women's rights.

Many development theorists and commentators employ economic definitions of globalisation (for example, Wanyeki 2004; Kelly 2004; Makhlouf 2004). As Desai (2004) observes, however, globalisation has space, time and cognitive dimensions. In terms of the latter, it is more than economic ideas that circulate. Cornwall and Nyamu-Musembi (2004), for example, reveal the antecedents of rights-based approaches to development, their transfer from local/national to global forums, and their various manifestations in different places and among different development actors. Globalisation can therefore be conceived more broadly than being just the worldwide circulation of particular economic policies and their concomitant cultural forms. Globalisation also involves the worldwide circulation of ideas about rights, democracy, education, peace, activism, strategies, philsosophies and so on, and studies in globalisation rightly include studies of social movements and transnational advocacy. It is pertinent, therefore, to view the growth and development of a local grassroots NGO such as Leitana Nehan as a positive aspect of the phenomenon of globalisation, and it is worth exploring how Leitana Nehan has become embedded in a web of networks.

Henry et al. (2004) argue that networks are transnational agents of development. They assert that networks arise primarily in response to the challenges of global capital and information and communication technologies, and that networks help to improve an organisation's competitive advantage. In the case of Leitana Nehan, its networks developed as a result of a need to promote peace-building in Bougainville, and the organisation was not so much interested in competitive advantage as in finding ways to achieve their goals. Other aspects of the ideas of Henry et al. (2004) about networks are, however, worth employing here as a lens through which to analyse Leitana Nehan's work. First, they argue that understanding networks involves understanding the power dynamics involved, and the inclusions and exclusions that occur in the process of establishing networks. Second, Henry et al. (2004) advocate the examination of how networks are established and maintained, and the commonalities and contestations of values inherent in and influencing the networks. Below, I explore these two dimensions of the networks that Leitana Nehan has established, after first attempting to map their development over the three periods of Leitana Nehan's history described in Chapters 2–5.

LEITANA NEHAN'S NETWORKS

Drawing on material in previous chapters of this book, I now attempt to show how the characteristics and dynamics of the networks in which Leitana Nehan is enmeshed have developed and changed over time. Some social network analysts attempt to measure the strength of relationships in social networks (Wasserman and Pattison 2004; Freeman 2005), but the descriptions provided in the previous chapters indicate the extent to which Leitana Nehan has been involved with various actors. Therefore, in this analysis I trace the changes and continuities in the types of groups with which Leitana Nehan has been involved, the geographical positioning of the group, and the kind of relationship that Leitana Nehan had with each group. I identify four broad groups: non-government organisations, including local, national, regional and international; governments, including local, provincial, national (PNG) and international (for example, Australia, Britain), as well as bodies comprising personnel from regional nations (for example, the Truce Monitoring Group); multilateral organisations (for example, UN bodies); and other social institutions (family, church, chiefly system). I use four geographical categories: Bougainville (including all of the province of Bougainville); Papua New Guinea (excluding Bougainville); the region (including Australia, New Zealand, the South Pacific islands) and the rest of the world. I group relationships into four broad kinds. I recognise that relationships can be multidimensional, and I attempt to identify the major kind of relationship that occurred between Leitana Nehan and the other groups. The relationships are

- providing Leitana Nehan with funding for programs for community members
- providing Leitana Nehan staff or volunteers with funding for training or directly providing training or professional development, including conference attendance and study tours
- providing logistical or material support, such as equipment, transport, or personnel for joint delivery of programs
- moral support and legitimacy, such as the support provided by families and other women's organisations or the legitimacy afforded by prizes.

Furthermore, I compare these relationships across the three periods of Leitana Nehan's history that I employed in Chapters 2–5, namely, 1992–95 (pre Beijing); 1995–99; and 2000–04.

In the period 1992–95, most of the components of Leitana Nehan's network were within Bougainville. Given that the crisis was at its peak, this is not surprising. The network within Bougainville comprised family, friends, the church and the chiefly system, which provided moral support and legitimacy, as well as logistical and material support. Some logistical support and professional development was obtained through the provincial government, and its affiliate, the Provincial Council of Women. The network comprised some links with other parts of Papua New Guinea, including the Rabaul Diocese of the Catholic Church, which assisted with supplies of second-hand clothes; the BEST group, who provided training for local women; and the Goroka office of SCF, which supplied medicines for distribution. In the region, Leitana Nehan linked with two Australian NGOs, namely IWDA and CAA, which provided training and funding.

In the period 1995–99, Leitana Nehan's network expanded considerably in particular directions, especially once the ceasefire came into effect in 1997. The cessation of hostilities allowed greater levels of communication, although there continued to be risks involved. Most of the components of the network within Bougainville remained intact. Leitana Nehan began to make more contact with other Bougainville-based NGOs, particularly in terms of liaison and exchange of ideas, which enhanced the legitimacy of their work. The organisation also began to have contacts with a much wider range of NGOs in Australia, New Zealand and the Pacific, as well as the wider world. These included Community Aid Abroad, IWDA, Oxfam NZ, Pacific Women Against Violence Network, Fiji Women's Crisis Centre, the Asian and Pacific Development Centre, World Vision, Caritas, Oxfam, SCF, and the YWCA. These connections mainly involved the provision to Leitana Nehan of funding and training or professional development. In addition to this extensive expansion of Leitana Nehan's NGO network, the organisation made links with a much wider range of governments and government bodies in this time. In Bougainville, it continued to have contacts with the Bougainville provincial governments, and also made contact with the BRA at one stage. In Papua New Guinea, it had dealings with the Division of Health, and commenced its work with the National Broadcasting Corporation. The organisation had dealings with the Truce Monitoring Group and its successor, the Peace Monitoring Group, as well as with AusAID and the British High Commission. Although Leitana Nehan continued to have contacts with the Catholic church in both Bougainville and the remainder of Papua New Guinea, there appear to have been few, if any, links with church bodies outside Papua New Guinea—in contrast to the situation with its contacts with NGOs and governments. Furthermore, in this period, there were few, if any, formal links with multilateral organisations such as UNICEF, UNESCO, WHO or other UN bodies.

From 2000 onwards, during the Strengthening Communities for Peace project, Leitana Nehan continued to expand its networks on Bougainville and beyond. Its networks among chiefs, the local churches, and local NGOs remained intact, and their relations with these groups were of a similar kind. New links developed with NGOs, governments and international organisations in various parts of the world. However, three major changes in the type and characteristics of Leitana Nehan's positioning stand out. First, its links with outside NGOs became more intently focused on its relationship with IWDA, because of the partnership with that organisation (described in Chapters 4, 5 and 7).

This was inevitable because of the substantial size of the Strengthening Communities for Peace project, which was on a scope and scale well beyond any previous work conducted by Leitana Nehan. As Jonathan Makuwira noted in Chapter 7, the nature of the relationship between these two NGOs shifted over time, from one of client–beneficiary to one of relative mutuality, as the skills, experience and knowledge of Leitana Nehan leaders expanded.

Second, the nature of the relationship between Leitana Nehan and local and national NGOs shifted in this period. Initial contacts, such as with the Bougainville Women for Peace and Freedom, involved sharing experiences and establishing relationships (Chapter 3). Later, Leitana Nehan began offering some workshops jointly with other local NGOs. Starting in 2001, the executive director of Leitana Nehan began acting as a consultant to, or providing training for, other national, regional and international NGOs or funding bodies, such as NZ Aid, the Papua New Guinea Community Development Scheme, World Vision, and the Fiji Women's Crisis Centre. Whereas Leitana Nehan had in the past been a recipient of funds and other forms of support from such organisations, the organisation was now able to offer services to these organisations, based on experiences it had built up over a decade or more of community-based peace and development work.

The third notable change in the nature and characteristics of Leitana Nehan's networks in the period from 2000 concerned its relationship with Bougainville government bodies. In 1999, a single Bougainville provincial government was formed, replacing the Bougainville Interim Government and the Bougainville Transitional Government. Along with the continuation of the ceasefire, this allowed the re-establishment of various government functions such as police, the judiciary, the health system, the school system and so on. As a result, new opportunities arose for Leitana Nehan to expand its networks to connect with these groups. As was the case with the changes in Leitana Nehan's relationships with other NGOs, the new relationships with these government bodies involved more giving than receiving, particularly in the form of gender awareness and conflict transformation training for nurses, police, magistrates, and teachers.

EPILOGUE

Helen Hakena and Agnes Titus

After SCP2 finished in March 2004, our workload decreased dramatically. Nevertheless, we obtained a small amount of funds (K95,000) from the PNG Community Development Scheme for a number of projects. First, we extended and furnished the Leitana Nehan offices behind DJL Enterprises in Buka. Four more rooms were added, which are used for administration, counselling, and the Women's and Children's Referral Desk, and one is rented by an MP, providing a small amount of revenue.

The purpose of the Women's and Children's Referral Desk is to consolidate all the counselling services provided by NGO and government agencies. It provides an avenue for victims of violence to get help in a neutral, safe and friendly setting. We counsel them and, where needed, we contact the police to come and take the victim's statement and the doctor to come and examine the victim. The doctor will write out a statement. Cases then go to the courts. We have a twenty-four hour service. Counsellors help with other women's issues as well, such as maintenance claims by deserted or single mothers.

Second, the CDS funds were used for awareness workshops in three communities or schools in each of the 13 districts. However, the funds did not allow us to do any follow-up workshops. Many primary schools had undergone a top-up process which involved adding grades 7 and 8 to the existing 6 grades. However, many schools noticed that bullying had increased during this process, so the CDS-funded workshops in schools specifically focused on bullying issues and children's rights.

Third, the radio program continued weekly, with a particular emphasis on sexual violence and child abuse, as well as programs educating people about issues relevant to the election of the Autonomous Bougainville Government (ABG), since the election was due in the first half of 2005. Topics covered included good governance and leadership qualities. We received lots of verbal feedback from individuals on the topics presented. Then, after the ABG's inauguration, the radio program presented the topic, '*lukluk bek*' or evaluation of the election process. Again, we received some very positive feedback from a number of individuals.

Fourth, we used the CDS funds to do some community development training, including community mapping. We held two training workshops—one in Tsiroge (for north Bougainville), which George Lesi conducted before becoming ill, and one in Arawa (for south and central).

Helen was nominated to be organiser of National Literacy Week in October 2004, in her role as Chair of the Provincial Literacy Committee. The committee received K70,000 funding from the PNG Department of Education. We used K40,000 to launch national literacy week in Tinputz, and K30,000 to host the closing ceremony in Buin.

Although no funds were available for these programs, Helen conducted training for police and hospital staff in Buka on gender awareness, domestic violence and other women's issues, and for women at Kekesu in Tinputz on women's rights. We have been facilitating youth training in our own time, such as with the Hanpan Youth Organisation. We also participated in meetings with other NGOs and women's groups to plan 16 days of activism countering violence against women from 25 November–10 December 2004. During this period we were involved in marking World AIDS Day, World Human Rights Day, and World Disability Day, among others. During these celebrations, the Hihatuts and Youth to Youth theatre troupes performed and speeches were made. Funding came from various sources, such as the Bougainville AIDS council, while we also used the radio program to reinforce some of these topics at the time.

During 2004, a local grade 7 student was raped and later died of her injuries. The perpetrator was known to the community, but was being protected by his family. We organised a march in protest against the inaction of the police, and submitted a petition to the government. This forced the police to arrest the perpetrator, who is now serving a long gaol term.

We were involved in a range of cross-sectoral meetings. We attended a forward-looking meeting for Bougainville NGOs in Arawa to discuss how the NGO sector and ABG could support each other. We also attended meetings of the Consultation, Implementation and Monitoring Council, a body of the PNG National Executive Council, when it met in Rabaul. In addition, the islands region recommended that Agnes present their recommendations at the National Development Forum at Parliament House in Port Moresby.

Funding limitations have restricted the amount of international networking that we have been able to do. Nevertheless, Kris went to a workshop on non-violence and social empowerment in Orissa, India, and in June 2005 he attended a seminar in the Netherlands on 'Security When the State Fails', presenting a paper outlining a case study of Ieta village, which was completely burnt down during the crisis (see Chapter 2).

During 2004 we were successful in our proposal to NZ Aid for K380,000 in funds to continue the various counselling programs in Buka and in the districts. Although we hoped to start in 2004, the first tranche of project funds were only acquitted in February 2005, which meant that the project would not run until February 2006. While we were waiting for the funding to arrive, the Fiji Women's Crisis Centre conducted a 'Basic Counselling' workshop in Buka. The NZ funds have been used to support two counsellors (usually one male and one female) in each district. Most of these counsellors had already been trained as part of, and worked in, the SCP projects, so they already knew about relevant issues and strategies. They live in their own homes, but work closely with the nurses in the sub-health centres in the districts, and identify a specific day when they are available in the health centres. This provides women who report domestic violence issues an opportunity to see a counsellor as well as a nurse. The counsellors also see clients in other places, such as their own homes, and neighbouring villages and constituencies. They sometimes sit in on court cases in the districts, especially those involving women's issues. The locations of the counsellors have been advertised through the radio program and in letters to district managers and local churches. The radio program is also used to inform people about other agencies that provide counselling and related services, although most of these services are based in Buka. Unfortunately, the districts are large, and people cannot always access the counsellors. For major problems or legal issues, clients are referred to the Buka Leitana Nehan office counsellors. Bianca Hakena and Elizabeth Behis, the senior counsellors in Buka, also travel to the districts to support the counsellors. Nevertheless, the NZ Aid funds have made a large difference to the extent to which we have been able to provide counselling services. In the last 12 months of the SCP 2, we averaged 55 clients per month. In the 12 months from when the SCP finished and the NZ funds became available, we saw an average of 12 clients per month. In the last seven whole months that the NZ funds have been available, we have seen an average of 53 clients per month.

One of the major activities for 2005 involved Agnes' campaign for the northern region women's seat in the election for the ABG. We travelled around many parts of the region meeting people in communities and talking about the ABG and various issues. It was a learning experience for us, but also we used the campaign talks to educate people about what to expect from the ABG. There were good turn-outs everywhere we went, and we used our networks to publicise meetings, and many Leitana Nehan volunteers provided translation services in their communities. Some volunteers also promoted our campaign in their home area. This helped reduce costs. We did not campaign in Kunua because we did not have much of a network there, but it is a big area and not campaigning there probably cost Agnes votes. The communities we visited really respected us. We received no verbal abuse like some of the male candidates did. People did not hold anything against us. The chiefs in particular were very respectful. Some of the chiefs standing in the individual constituencies also helped us out and had joint meetings. Sometimes we would give these chiefs a lift in our vehicle, whereas the male candidates did not tend to help each other out in this way.

After Francisca Semoso won the north region women's seat, Helen organised for all the female candidates to come to the Leitana Nehan office so that Sharon Rolls from Femlink (Fiji) could interview them. They shared their experiences about campaigning. Agnes maintained a good relationship with Francisca because they campaigned together.

During the campaign we knew more about the issues than the men, and were able to speak about them. During the campaign we did not make any promises, because we knew what the ABG would face. We talked mainly about the fact that the peace agreement allows for the gradual drawing down of power from the national government to the ABG, and the fact that the ABG would not have many powers to start with. We realised that many people did not understand this aspect of the peace process and the move to autonomy. Even some of the candidates were making promises that they would not be able to deliver, because of the nature of the peace agreement and the gradual move to taking over national powers. Now that the ABG is in place, people are noticing that it is really moving very slowly—they are sitting on the same spot. As a candidate, Agnes was not unhappy about losing because she now realises that Leitana Nehan has the capacity as an organisation outside the government to support the winning and losing women candidates and to continue to educate them about women's issues and good governance. We can also support women in general, and continue to negotiate with the government. We have a very good relationship with Francisca, and the Minister for Women, NGOs, Youth, and churches and local level Government, Magdelene Toroansi.

Another good thing about this campaign was that all the women candidates for the north region would go to one community together to campaign. They would each take turns speaking, and then the voters could make up their own minds.

Some candidates were promising large pots of money, as if it would be like the national MPs' discretionary funding, but we told the people that no such thing would exist in the ABG. We had realised through the SCP that it is important to educate people and tell them the truth, because many people are not aware of how the system works or how the wider world connects. With our connections, we can assist the three women members. They are learning a lot from us. Recently, for example, we had a meeting with them about women's issues in the province, and informed them about some local controversies.

We were very sad when our long-time colleague and assistant executive director George Lesi died in August 2004. He was committed and always put other people first. He was not selfish with his time or skills, and he was a very good mentor for us. We learned so much from him. We haven't been able to find anyone like him who was always there for other people, and always doing things with people so that they learned and took on the responsibility. He was never overpowering, but always guiding and giving us time to do things. He always encouraged us to find our own solutions and to think through the issues.

In March 2005 we advertised the position of assistant executive director. Four people applied, and the successful candidate was Agnes Titus, our team leader from Nissan. She took up the position after the election, in May 2005.

In Bougainville, the NGO sector is becoming very strong. In the north we have an umbrella organisation known as BACDA; in central Bougainville, Nikana Matara serves this function; and in south they have the Southwest Alliance of Community Development. In the north, we are now planning an NGO show-and-tell for donors and the government, profiling the members of BACDA, which consists of Leitana Nehan, the Adventist Development and Relief Agency (ADRA), the Bougainville Interchurch Women's Forum (BICWF), Peace Foundation Melanesia, Bougainville Trauma Institute, Bougainville AIDS Council, Bougainville Microfinance, Caritas PNG, Callan Services, Catholic Family Life, World Vision and Bougainville Provincial Council of Women. The idea is for each NGO to share its work, objectives, history, and who they are, hoping that when the donors and government hear what we do, we can work better together and strengthen links with donors and government.

We have continued our advocacy work. For example, recently there was a strong debate about women and girls wearing trousers and shorts. On one occassion, about six women from Haku came to the office. They were not just ordinary women, but leaders and chiefs. They said, 'Mrs Hakena, we have a problem in Haku. The men and chiefs in Haku are saying we should not wear trousers. It is against culture and against religion'.

Soon after, some other women from Wakunai came into the office. They told us that the council of chiefs in Wakunai had had a meeting and decided to impose a K50 fine on women wearing trousers. When she heard this second report, we notified Goretty Kenneth, a Buka-based reporter for the *Post-Courier* newspaper in Port Moresby, and we also sent a press release to Radio Bougainville, who carried the story on their news. Our press release pointed out that it was unconstitutional for men to discriminate against women in this way. After it was on the radio, three more women came from Gogohe and said that a politician had gathered the chiefs and told them that women should not be wearing trousers. Soon after, some women from Petats came to the office and said that three years ago they had been banned from wearing trousers and that those unable to pay the K50 fine were made to cut grass. Agnes went down to the police station to see the officer in charge of keeping records of complaints. She asked how many women had complained about having to pay the fines and discovered that seven such cases had been reported to the police already. After the media release, three women came from Pokpok Island and stated that they had each been made to pay a K50 fine for wearing trousers a year earlier. Also, after hearing the radio announcement, women from Siwai, who had been wearing trousers under their laplaps, started wearing them on the outside and came up to Buka to thank them for exposing the issue. Then, an MP, whose wife was one of the first to come to Leitana Nehan and complain, came and said the chiefs were going to take Helen to court or else demand a pig. He reported that the chiefs said that Helen should not talk about all the UN conventions, because we are here in Buka and we can make our own laws.

These kinds of patriarchal attitudes to women are still common. Recently, Agnes went to Kunua with the police and the AIDS council for a training workshop. There were 124 people present, including students, community people and community auxiliary police. One of the men got up and said, 'you know with regards to rape, it's you women who must be careful to dress in a way that does not attract men. You women are too fancy, you pluck your eyebrows and wear dangly earrings', and he went on and on. Agnes got up and said to the audience, and especially that man, 'if your body is attracted to earrings, then go and rape the earrings, don't rape the woman. If the clothes excite you, rape the clothes, don't rape the body. We are against rape because you rape our bodies and do a lot of damage to us. This idea about women being the cause of rape is not true. Just because you hear it, doesn't mean it is true. Even women who are wearing grubby clothes, or who are small children, get raped'.

Many of the team leaders and members from SCP have gone on to take on other leadership roles in their communities. Dorcas Tutou, the team leader from Siwai, is training to become an elementary school teacher. Anne Rangai, the former project officer, is a counsellor as well as a district women's facilitator for the Education Department. Paul Kauori, the deputy team leader from Paruparu, is now a counsellor and a male nurse in that area. Ezekial Lames, who was the team leader for Northwest district, has his own theatre troupe, Youth To Youth, which is raising awareness of HIV/AIDS and domestic violence. Fabian Kotsin is still the director of Hihatuts Theatre Troupe, but was a field worker for CDS for six years, and is now also working as a volunteer for UNICEF. Susan Pakoi is a district women's facilitator and chair of the Buin's Women's Council and secretary of the Provincial Council of Women. Laura Ampa, formerly a team member in Buin district, is now a parliamentary member for the south regional seat. Stanley Pakita from Tinputz facilitated the community development training with George Lesi in 2004, and now works as a volunteer with World Vision on an *ad hoc* basis doing community mapping. Benedicta Noneng, one of the project officers, has started a kindergarten in Arawa, while Rose Trongat is secretary of the Catholic Women's Association for Gogohe as well as for the Bougainville diocese as a whole. Joy Vanahe, a counsellor, went on to become a community health nurse. Although many of our former volunteers have gone their separate ways, many of them still maintain a sense of solidarity with each other and support each other when they can. They drop into the Leitana Nehan office, and support our work when they can. They are like a family.

Even today, when funding is a bit slow in getting to us, we are still working to our full capacity. We enjoy the work. We love working with our communities. We are affected by what happens in our communities. Therefore, we must continue the community development work because we want to see and enjoy peace.

APPENDIXES

Appendix 1 Staff and volunteers, 1992–99

Abel Willy
Agnes Titus
Alex Bunn
Alexia Samo
Alina Longa
Andrew Goman
Anne Rangai
Audrey Katia
Belgin Tsivele
Benedicta Noneng
Bianca Hakena
Bosco Bunn
Brenda Tohiana
Cecilia Francis
Cecilia Sinato
Chris Rere
Chris Sagolo
Clement Borats
Dalton Towasa
David Vengiau
Delphine Lesi
Delphine Tsigoto
Delphine Wasas
Dominic Morokonu
Eileen Kirama
Elizabeth Behis
Elizabeth Skoi
Ezekiel Lames
Fabian Kotsin
Felix Brian
Finan Balei
Francis Botsia
Francis Kera
Gemma Goman
George Lesi
Getsi Luke
Yvonne Baito

Gordon Gunan
Grace Rumana
Gregory Tagu
Helen Hakena
Helen Kamits
Hendry Saris (Fr)
Henry Bosin
Hillary. K. Laris
Jennifer Hasop
Jessica Symanen
Jessie Walo
John Kiha
Julius Longa
Justinian Suraka
Kebon Boniface
Kris Hakena
Leonard Mokela
Leonard Tsitoa
Linus Saram
Lydia Tasa
Marceline Semoso
Maria Nahi
Matilda Korus
Michael Titus
Norman Tola
Patrick Tsikoa
Pauline Nawan
Petra Rangei
Quentin Hotsia
Regina Ratson
Roger Tukana
Rose Trongat
Samson Lino
Steven Kuta
Thomas Kunu
Tony Bovora
Valentine Tur

Appendix 2   Strengthening Communities for Peace project, 2000–04: volunteer teams and communities

DISTRICT	COMMUNITIES	VOLUNTEERS
BUKA TEAM	Lemanmanu Primary School	Valentine Tur (M)
	Lontis Primary School	Maria Nahi (F)
	Kohia Community	Belgine Tsivele (F)
	Ielelina Community	Allen Tsikula (M)
	Hanahan Primary School	Quentine Hotsia (M)
	Nova Community	Theresa Tarihun (F)
	Pororan Community	Raymond Hareke (M)
	Ieta Community	
	Hangan Community	
	Lose Community	
	Gogohe School	
	Sohano Community and School	
	Hutjena Secondary School	
	Hamatana School	
NISSAN TEAM	Gerei Community	Agnes Titus (F)
	Tuhus Community	Peter Hensi (M)
	Kulis Community	Ludwina Baki (F)
	Yotsibol Community	Kevin Perengi (M)
	Holy Cross High School	Polynarius Maton (M)
	Sigon Primary School	Loretta Titus (F)
	Mapiri Community & School	Nerry Libika (F)
	Balil 1, 2 and 3 Community	
	Mantoia Community	
	Tanamalit Community	
	Tanaheran Community	
	Tapongal Community	
	Tabanglek Community	
	Mantoia Community	
SELAU/SUIR TEAM	Hahon Primary School	Demondford Sali (M)
	Sorom Community & Primary School	Elizabeth Katoa (F)
		Grace Tsiarno (F)
	Tarlena High School	Gregory Tagu (M)
	Tekokni Primary School	Helen Kamits (F)
	Tsunpets Community	Joe Kenehata (M)
	Manob Community	Clement Borats (M)
	Gohi Community	
	Tiloa School & Community	
	Baniata Community	
	Tsundawan Community	
	Tabut Community	
	Arabia Community	

	Soakela Community	
	Tsiroge Community	
	Metu Community	
TINPUTZ TEAM	Teosipota Primary School	Stanley Pakita (M)
	Tearuki Community School	Philip Hulasoho (M)
	Pusoer Community	Sandra Rapitai (F)
	Irue Community	Linus Rapitai (M)
	Tinputz Primary School	Gethrude Koanan (F)
	Teabes Community	Gregory Tasino (M)
	Pokapa 1 and 2 Communities	Eugene Revin (M)
	Tiop Community	Joylene Vanahe (F)
	Iokomori Community	
	Puskot Community	
	Wagog Community	
NORTHWEST TEAM	Saposa Primary School	Herman Siriva (M)
	Amun Community	Mark Vutsimbo (M)
	Kostawan Primary School	Jean Tsiniu (F)
	Sipai Primary School	Susan Poto (F)
	Atsinima Community	Rufina Arave (F)
	Pukuito Community	Geraldine Sinato (F)
	Mapisi Station	Ezekial Lames (M)
	Bishop Wade Secondary School	
	Torokina School & Community	
	Piva Community	
	Koiare Community	
	Hon Community	
	Taiof Community	
	Kereaka Community	
WAKUNAI TEAM	Inus Community	Geoffrey Micah (M)
	Itae Primary School	Judith Hinnah (F)
	Teohiup Community	Monica Kusa (F)
	Kepesia Primary School	Hilary Hutchin (M)
	Turima Primary School	Albert Taveakoro (M)
	Aita Community	Gillian Paul (F)
	Asitavi Secondary School	Nancy Petrus (F)
	Wakunai Station & Primary School	Samuel Palavi (M)
MANETAI TEAM	Manetai Primary School	Meisy Gaviato (F)
	Kopani 2 Community	Susan Pasia (F)
	Popee Community School	Benedicta Deku (F)
	Bana High School	Patricia Duffy (F)
	Pele Primary School	Grace Kerepas (F)
		Raymond Bele (M)
		Florence Gabiato (F)

PARUPARU TEAM	Darinai Primary School	John Ibouko (M)
	Paruparu Primary School	Paul Kauori (M)
	Konuku SDA Station	Veronica Taruito (F)
	Kossia Community	Assumpta Navo (F)
	Waruwaru Community	Francis Manomo (M)
		Josephine Tarurate (F)
		Agnes (F)
		Francisca Pereira (F)
KOROMIRA/	Koianu Primary School	Dominic Morokonu (M)
KOIANU TEAM	Sirivai/Makasi Community	Willie Sive (M)
	Siorovi Community	Elijah Kanare (M)
	Take Community	Fatima Morokonu (F)
	Tuarerukung Community	Tony Bovora (M)
		David Vengiau (M)
		Timothy Karove (M)
SIWAI TEAM	Pataiku Community	Dorcas Tutou (F)
	Sininai Primary School	Ruth Autahe (F)
	Kinirui Community	Mary Konong (F)
	Panakei Community	Sabina Motoi (F)
	Tonu Primary School	Isaac Pinomu (M)
		Moses Komon (M)
		Jacklyn Gamini (F)
BUIN TEAM	Pariro Community	Tony Kaupa (M)
	Ikulasi Community	Susan Pakoi (F)
	Tuitui Community	Margaret Beta (F)
	Maluatu Community	Steven Minsipi (M)
	Laguai Primary School	Raphael Tsiko (M)
		Joe Nakota (M)
		Paul Tomitom (M)
BANA TEAM	Konkopine Primary School	Cathy Kukui (F)
	Popee Community School	Mark Taivigi (M)
	Bana High School	Maggie Nampoa (F)
	Pele Primary School	Augustine Sagama (M)
		Elizabeth Tagusi (F)
		Rose Kobuko (F)
		Stepani Rohus (M)
		Thomas Kobuko (M)
TOROKINA TEAM	Kawatsia Elementary School	Rose Saimos (F)
	Reini Community	Joyce Ulapiri (F)
	Marowa Community	Wilfred Loma (M)
	Kawatsia Community	Lucy Mevetsi (F)
	Kenaia	Apolonia Barako (F)
		Charles Tsivo (M)
		Lemay Wakana (M)

Note: Phase 1 teams—15 communities; Phase 2 teams—5 communities

Appendix 3 Leitana Nehan Field Counsellors, 2005–06

DISTRICT	COUNSELLORS
Buka	Rose Trongat and Celestine Bubun
Nissan	Loretta Titus and Boniface Marutsi
Selau/Suir	Demondford Sali and Elizabeth Katoa
Northwest	Herman Sirivi and Gabriel Dosi
Tinputz	Stanley Pakita and Linus Saram
Wakunai	Geoffrey Micah and Samuel Palavi
Manetai	Grace Kerepas and Raymond Bele
Paruparu	John Ibouko and Paul Kauori
Koromira/Koianu	Fatima Morokonu and Francis Bove
Siwai	Dorcas Tutou and Anne Rangai
Buin	Susan Pakoi and Tony Kaupa
Torokina	Wilfred Loma and Charles Tsibo
Bana	Rose Kobuko and Michael Aganai

Appendix 4 Leitana Nehan Board Members, 1997–2005

Name	Position and term of office
Agnes Titus	Chair, 1997–99
Josephine Taria	Member, 1997–
Julius Longa	Member, 1997–2000
Fr Boniface Kevon	Member, 1997–2000
Celine Kiroha	Chair, 1999–2000; Member, 1997–2000
Helen Hakena	Ex-officio Member, 1999–2000
Celesta Soagai	Member, 1999–2000
Severina Muta	Member, 1999–2000
Mona Kakarouts	Chair, 2000–
Josephine Gatana	Member, 2000–
Fidelis Dana	Member, 2000–
Michael Katoa	Member, 2000–
Apolonia Sanga	Member, 2000–
Carol Hon	Member, 2000–
Jacky Niniku	Member, 2000–
Dolly Lalu	Member, 2000–

Appendix 5   Radio program topics, 2000–05

Radio Program No.	Topic
2000	
1	*Domestic Violence Emi Wanem Samting* (What is domestic violence)
2	Violence against Women *na* [and] Male Violence against Women
3	Violence against Women
4	Violence against Women
5	Violence
6	Violence
7	Domestic Violence
8	Domestic Violence
9	Domestic Violence
10	Domestic Violence
11	*Risins Watpo Domestic Violence Ikamap* (Reasons behind domestic violence)
12	*Bai Yumi Mekim Wanem long Stopim Domestic Violence* (What can we do to prevent domestic violence)
13	*Hombru Alcohol na ol Bagarap Emi Kamap long ol Husat i Dringim* (Home brewed alcohol and the problems that arise from drinking it)
14	*Hombru Alcohol na ol Bagarap i Save Kamap* (Problems arising from home brewed alcohol)
15	*Wantaim ol Travol na Bagarap i Kamap long Pasin Blong Dringim Alcohol Olsem Hombru* (Problems arising from homebrew consumption)
16	*Hombru* (Home brewed alcohol)
17	*Wanem Samting Em i Defense Mechanism?* (What is a defence mechanism?)
18	Defence Mechanism
19	Defence Mechanism
20	Defence Mechanism
21	*Sampela Wei, Tingting na ol Idea Man Inap Usim O Helpim Em long Noken Huk long Alcohol* (Ways and ideas for avoiding alcohol addiction)
22	Alcohol (continued)
2001	
23	*Painim Solution bilong Alcoholic Problem Emi Gat* (How to solve your alcohol problem)
24	Alcohol
25	*Radio Program ol i Kolim long Strengthening Communities For Peace* (The Strengthening Communities for Peace radio program)
26	*Wanem Samting Em i Rape?* (What is rape?)

60	Integral Human Development
61	Integral Human Development
62	The Church and the Work of Promoting Justice and Peace
63	*Wanpela Rot Yumi Mas Bihainim long Pinisim ol Kros, Tokpait Insait long ol Community bilong Yumi* (What we need to do to overcome anger and verbal abuse in our communities)
64	Human Rights

2003

1	*Toktok bilong Holy Father, Pope John Paul 2 i Bin Redim long Makim Lent 2002* (Words from the Holy Father, Pope John Paul II, at Lent, 2002)
2	*Toktok bilong Pope John Paul 2* (Speech by Pope John Paul II)
3	*Corruption na Kain Leadership Yumi Mas Lukluk longen long 2002 National Election* (Corruption and the kind of leadership we need to seek in the 2002 election)
4	*Corruption na Kain Leadership Yumi Mas Lukluk longen long 2002 National Election* (Corruption and the kind of leadership we need to seek in the 2002 election)
5	*Noken Votim Tru Candidate Emi Korapt* (Don't vote for corrupt candidates)
6	*Votim o Makim Lida Husat Bai Nap Mekim ol Gutpela Wok bilong Yumi* (Voting for and identifying leaders who can do good work for us)
7	*Votim o Makim Lida Husat Bai Nap Mekim ol Gutpela Wok bilong Yumi Yumi* (Voting for and identifying leaders who can do good work for us)
8	*Votim o Makim Lida Husat Bai Nap Mekim ol Gutpela Wok bilong Yumi Yumi* (Voting for and identifying leaders who can do good work for us)
9	*Votim ol Responsible Leader* (Voting for responsible leaders)
10	Making or Breaking Papua New Guinea in this Election
11	Translating the Language of Good Governance

2004

1	Pre Election Strategies (Qualities)
2	Pre Election Strategies (Qualities
3	Pre Election Strategies (Qualities)
4	Pre Election Strategies—*Noken Pas long Wanpela Kain Idea o Tingting*
5	Pre Election—Getting Started
6	Pre Election
7	Pre Election Strategies Sexual Violence/Child Abuse
8	Pre Election Strategies Sexual Violence/Child Abuse
9	Pre Election Strategies Sexual Violence/Child Abuse
10	Pre Election Strategies

2005

1	Acknowledgements, AusAID, NZ Aid, Radio Bougainville and the

REFERENCES

Ahai, N.G. 1999, 'Grassroots development vision for New Bougainville', in G. Harris, N. Ahai and R. Spence (eds), *Building Peace in Bougainville*, University of New England, Armidale:113–138.

Alpers, P., 2005. *Gun-Running in Papua New Guinea: from arrows to assault weapons in the Southern Highlands,* Small Arms Survey, Geneva.

Angeles, L., 2003. 'Creating social spaces for transnational feminist advocacy: The Canadian International Development Agency, the National Commission on the Role of Filipino Women, and Philippine women's NGOs', *The Canadian Geographer*, 47(3): 283–302.

Barter, P., 2004. 'Matters of concern in the Panguna No-Go Zone', *Post Courier*, 25 August.

Bennett, J., 1997, 'Introduction', in J. Bennett (ed.), *NGOs and Government: a review of current practice for Southern and Eastern NGOs,* INTRAC, London:1–12.

——, 2000. 'Across the Bougainville Strait: commercial interests and colonial reality, c. 1880–1960', *The Journal of Pacific History*, 35(1):67–82.

Blackwood, B., 1979. *Both Sides of Buka Passage: an ethnographic study of social, sexual and economic questions in the North-Western Solomon Islands*, AMS Press, New York.

Böge, V. and Garasu, Sr. L., 2004. 'Papua New Guinea: a success story of postconflict peacebuilding in Bougainville', in A. Heijmans, N. Simmonds, and H. van de Veens (eds), *Searching for Peace in Asia Pacific: an overviews of conflict prevention and peacebuilding activities,* Lynne Rienner Publishers, Boulder and London:564–80.

Brand-Jacobsen, K.F. and Jacobsen, C.G., 2000. 'Beyond mediation: towards more holistic approaches to peacebuilding and peace actor empowerment', in J. Galtung and C.G. Jacobsen (eds), *Searching for Peace: the road to transcend*, Pluto Press, London:231–67.

Brehm, V.M., 2001. *Promoting Effective North South NGO Partnerships: a comparative study of 10 European NGOs*, INTRAC Occasional Papers No. 35, INTRAC, London.

Byrne, T., 1983. *Integral Development: development of the whole person—a handbook for Christians*, Mission Press, Ndola, Zambia.

Carl, A., 2000. *Reflecting on Peace Practice Project: a case study*, Collaborative for Development Action, Cambridge, Massachusetts.

Chan-Tiberghien, J., 2004. *Gender and Human Rights Politics in Japan: global norms and domestic networks*, Stanford University Press, Stanford.

Chen Jie, 2001. 'Burgeoning transnationalism of Taiwan's social movement NGOs', *Journal of Contemporary China*, 10(29):613–44.

Claxton, K., 1998. *Bougainville 1988–1998: five searches for security in the North Solomons Province of Papua New Guinea*, Research School of Pacific and Asian Studies, The Australian National University, Canberra.

Cornwall, A. and Nyamu-Musembi, C., 2004. 'Putting the "rights-based approach" to development into perspective', *Third World Quarterly*, 25(8):1415–37.

Corry, B., 2002. 'The Bougainville peace process: the 'Pacific' settlement of disputes?', in Bruce Vaughan (ed.), *The Unraveling of Island Asia? Governmental, communal and regional instability*, Praeger, Westport, Connecticut:101–18.

Cox, E., 2004a. *Strengthening Communities for Peace Project: evaluation report*, Leitana Nehan Women's Development Agency, Buka, Bougainville.

——, 2004b. *Evaluation Report – Leitana Nehan Women's Development Agency's Strengthening Communities for Peace Project: Phase 2 – From Peace to Progress*, International Women's Development Agency, Melbourne.

Desai, M., 2004. 'Gender, health and globalization: a critical social movement perspective', *Development*, 47(2):36–42.

Dinnen, S., 1999. 'Militaristic solutions in a weak state: Internal security, private contractors, and political leadership in Papua New Guinea', *The Contemporary Pacific*, 11(2):279–303.

Dorney, S., 1998. *The Sandline Affair: politics and mercenaries and the Bougainville crisis*, ABC Books, Sydney.

Edwards, M., 1999. *Future Positive: international cooperation in the 21ˢᵗ century*, Earthscan, London.

Ewig, C., 1999. 'The strengths and limits of the NGO women's movement model: shaping Nicaragua's democratic institutions', *Latin American Research Review*, 34(3):75–102.

Fisher, J., 1993. *The Road to Rio: sustainable development and the non-governmental movement in the Third World*, Praeger, Westport, Connecticutt.

Fisher, S., 2004. Building a social theology for post-conflict recovery: rethinking reconciliation with special reference to Bougainville, PhD dissertation, University of New England, Armidale.

Fitzduff, M. and Church, C., 2004. 'Stepping up to the table: NGO strategies for influencing policy on conflict issues', in M. Fitzduff and C. Church (eds), *NGOs at the Table: strategies for influencing policies in areas of conflict*, Rowman and Littlefield, Lanham, Maryland:1–22.

Forster, M., 1992. 'The Bougainville Revolutionary Army', *The Contemporary Pacific*, 4(2):368–72.

Foucault, M., 1972. *The Archaeology of Knowledge*, Tavistock, London.

——, 1991. *Discipline and Punish: the birth of the prison*, Penguin Books, London.

Fowler, A., 1991. 'Building partnerships between Northern and Southern development NGOs: issues for the 1990s', *Development in Practice*, 1(1):5–18.

——, 1997. *Striking a Balance: a guide to enhancing the effectiveness of non-governmental organisations in international development*, Earthscan Publication, London.

——, 2000a. *Civil Society, NGDOs and Social Development: changing the rules of the game*, Occasional Papers No. 1, UN Research Institute for Social Development, Geneva.

——, 2000b. *Partnerships—Negotiating relationships: a resource for non-governmental development organisations,* INTRAC Occasional Papers No. 32, INTRAC, Oxford.

——, 2000c. *Questioning partnership: the reality of aid and NGO relations,* IDS Bulletin 31, Institute of Development Studies, Brighton.

Freeman, L.C., 2005. 'Graphic techniques for exploring social network data', in P.J. Carrington, J. Scott & S. Wasserman (eds), *Models and Methods in Social Network Analysis,* Cambridge University Press, New York:248–69.

Galama, A. and van Tongeren, P. (eds), 2002. *Towards Better Peacebuilding Practice,* European Centre for Conflict Prevention, Utrecht, Netherlands.

Garasu, L., 2002. 'The role of women in promoting peace and reconciliation', in A. Carl and L. Garasu (eds), *Weaving Consensus: the PNG–Bougainville peace process,* Accord 12, Conciliation Resources, London:n.p. Available online athttp://www.c-r.org/accord/boug/accord12/women.shtml

Ghai, Y. and Regan, A.J., 2002. 'Constitutional accommodation and conflict prevention', in A. Carl and L. Garasu (eds), *Weaving Consensus: the PNG–Bougainville peace process,* Accord 12, Conciliation Resources, London:n.p. Available online at http://www.c-r.org/accord/boug/accord12/constitutional.shtml.

Gidron, B., Kramer, R.M. and Salamon, E.M. (eds), 1992. *Government and the Third Sector: emerging relationships in welfare states,* Jossey-Bass Publications, San Francisco.

Hakena, H., 2002. 'Making Waves: Interview with Helen Hakena', *New Internationalist,* 350, October:n.p. Available online http://www.newint.org/issue350/waves.htm

——, 2003a. International Women's Day Speech, Sydney, 8 March. Available online at http://www.iwda.org.au/features/iwd2003/helen_speech.htm [accessed 31 March 2005]

——, 2003b. Lessons learned from the Bougainville crisis, Paper presented at the University of New England Peace Symposium, Armidale, 19–20 July.

——, 2005. 'Papua New Guinea: women in armed conflict', in R.

Baksh, L. Etchart, E. Onubogu and T. Johnson (eds), *Gender Mainstreaming in Conflict Transformation: building sustainable peace*, Commonwealth Secretariat, London:160–70.

Hannett, L., 1975. 'The case for Bougainville secession', *Meanjin Quarterly*, 34(3):286–93.

Harris, G., 1999. 'Reconstruction, recovery and development: the main tasks', in G. Harris (ed.), *Recovery from Armed Conflict in Developing Countries: an economic and political analysis*, Routledge, London:39–51.

—— and Lewis, N., 1999a. 'Structural violence, positive peace and peacebuilding', in G. Harris (ed.), *Recovery from Armed Conflict in Developing Countries: an economic and political analysis*, Routledge, London:29–35.

——, 1999b. 'Financing recovery and reconstruction, with particular reference to foreign assistance', in G. Harris (ed.), *Recovery from Armed Conflict in Developing Countries: An Economic and Political Analysis,* Routledge, London:111–28.

Havini, M., 1990. 'Perspectives on a crisis (3)', in P. Polomka (ed.), *Bougainville: Perspectives on a Crisis*, Strategic and Defence Studies Centre, Research School of Pacific and Asian Studies, Australian National University, Canberra: 17–27.

Henderson, J., 1999. 'Bougainville: the uncertain road to peace', *New Zealand International Review*, 24(3):10–13.

Henry, L., Mohan, G. and Yanacopulos, H.. 2004. 'Networks as transnational agents of development', *Third World Quarterly*, 25(5):839–55.

Hilhorst, D., 2003. *The Real World of NGOs: discourses, diversity and development*, Zed Books, London.

Howley, P., 2002. *Breaking Spears and Mending Hearts: peacemakers and restorative justice in Bougainville*, Zed Books and The Federation Press, London.

——, 2003. 'Restorative justice in Bougainville', in S. Dinnen (ed.), *A Kind of Mending: restorative justice in the Pacific Islands*, Pandanus Books, Canberra:215–54.

International Women's Development Agency (IWDA) n.d. Website, International Women's Development Agency, Melbourne. http:/

/www.ieda.org.au

INTRAC, 2001. *NGOs and Partnership*, NGO Policy Briefing Paper No. 4 For the NGO Sector Analysis Programme, Oxford: INTRAC.

Junne, G. and Verkoren, W., 2005. 'The challenges of post-conflict development', in G. Junne and W. Verkoren (eds), *Postconflict Development: meeting new challenges*, Lynne Reinner, Boulder:1–18.

Kabutaulaka, T., 1994. 'Cohesion and disorder in Melanesia: the Bougainville conflict and the Melanesian way', in W. vom Busch, M. Crocombe, R. Crocombe, L. Crowl, T. Delkin, P. Lamour and E. Williams (eds), *New Politics in the South Pacific*, Institute of Pacific Studies, University of the South Pacific, Rarotonga and Suva:63–82.

Korten, D., 1990. *Getting to the 21ˢᵗ Century: voluntary action and the global agenda*, Kumarian Press, West Hartford.

Layton, S., 1992. 'Fuzzy-wuzzy devils: mass media and the Bougainville crisis', *The Contemporary Pacific*, 4(2):299–323.

Leach, D.B.A., 1997. 'Models of inter-organisational collaboration in development', *Institutional Development*, 2(1):27–49.

Lederach, J.P., 1997. *Building Peace: sustainable reconciliation in divided societies*, United States Institute of Peace Press, Washington, DC.

——, 2005. *The Moral Imagination: the art and soul of building peace*, Oxford University Press, Oxford.

Lee, K., 2004. 'The pit and the pendulum: can globalization take health governance forward?', *Development*, 47(20):11–17.

Lewis, D., 2001. *The Management of Non-Governmental Organisations: an introduction*, Routledge, London.

Lewis, N., 1999a. 'Social recovery from armed conflict', in G. Harris (ed.), *Recovery from Armed Conflict in Developing Countries: an economic and political analysis*, Routledge, London:95–110.

——, 1999b. 'Women and children in the recovery process', in G. Harris (ed.), *Recovery from Armed Conflict in Developing Countries: an economic and political analysis*, Routledge, London:166–88.

Lister, S., 1999. *Power in Partnerships? An analysis of an NGO's relationships with its partners*, International Working Paper 5, London School of Economics, London. Available online at http:/

/www.lse.ac.uk/Deptss/ccs/pdf/int-work-paper5.pdf

LNWDA. 1997. Constitution of the Leitana Nehan Women's Development Agency.

——, 2000a. *1999 Annual Report*, LNWDA, Buka.

——, 2000b. *1st Quarterly Report - Strengthening Communities for Peace Project*, LNWDA, Buka.

——, 2000c. Submission to International Alert Women Building Peace Campaign. Section V.2, LNWDA, Buka.

——, 2000d. 2nd Quarterly Report - Strengthening Communities for Peace Project, LNWDA, Buka.

——, 2001a. *2000 Annual Report*, LNWDA, Buka.

——, 2001b. Brochure.

——, 2002a. *2001 Annual Report*, LNWDA, Buka.

——, 2002b. *3rd Quarterly Report - Strengthening Communities for Peace Project*, LNWDA, Buka.

——, 2002c. *4th Quarterly Report - Strengthening Communities for Peace Project*, LNWDA, Buka.

——, 2003a. Strengthening Communities for Peace through Good Governance: Strategic plan 2004-2007. Buka: LNWDA.

——, 2003b. Strengthening Communities for Peace: From Peace to Progress, Monthly Report, various issues, LNWDA, Buka.

——, 2003c. Strengthening Communities for Peace through Counselling - submitted to New Zealand Agency for International Development, Buka: LNWDA.

——, 2004. Strengthening Communities for Peace Through Good Governance, Strategic Plan 2004-2007, Buka: LNWDA.

——, n. d. Notable Events 1990–2003, LNWDA, Buka.

—— and IWDA, 1999. Strengthening Communities for Peace, Project Proposal submitted to AusAID Bougainville Reconstruction Program, LNWDA, Buka, and IWDA, Melbourne:.

——, 2001. Strengthening Communities for Peace: Year 2 Annual Plan, LNWDA, Buka, and IWDA, Melbourne.

Makhlouf, H.H., 2004. 'Globalization: the gap between promise and reality', *Journal of Development Alternatives and Area Studies*, 23(3/4):57–65.

Makuwira, J.J., 2003. Non-Governmental Organisations, Participation and Partnership Building in Basic Education in Malawi, PhD Thesis, University of New England.

Malhotra, K., 2000. 'NGOs without aid: beyond the global soup kitchen', *Third World Quarterly*, 21(4):655–68.

Martinussen, J.D. and Engberg-Pedersen, P., 2003. *Aid: understanding international cooperation,* Zed Books, London.

May, R.J., 2001. *State and Society in Papua New Guinea: the first twenty-five years,* Crawford House Publishing, Adelaide.

McMillan, S., 1998. 'Bringing peace to Bougainville', *New Zealand International Review*, 23(3):2–9.

Miriori, M., 2002. 'A Bougainville Interim Government (BIG) perspective on early peace efforts', in A. Carl and L. Garasu (eds), *Weaving Consensus: the PNG–Bougainville Peace Process,* Conciliation Resources, London:n.p. Available online at http://www.c-r.org/accord/boug/accord12/bougainville.shtml.

Namaliu, R., 1990. 'Perspectives on a Crisis (2)', in P. Polomka (ed.), *Bougainville: perspectives on a crisis,* Strategic and Defence Studies Centre, Research School of Pacific and Asian Studies, Australian National University, Canberra:13–16.

Ninnes, P., Jenkins, B., Harman, G., Spence, R., Mannam, M.A. and Lera, J., forthcoming. Higher Education and Post-Conflict Recovery: a Bougainville case study. Manuscript submitted to *International Journal of Peace Studies.*

Nwamuo, C., 2000. 'Capacity building through North–South partnerships: the African university sector', *Capacity.org: Advancing the Policy and Practice of Capacity Building in International Cooperation,* Capacity.org 6, Leiden.

O'Callaghan, M.L., 2002. 'The origin of the conflict', in A. Carl and L. Garasu (eds), *Weaving Consensus: the PNG–Bougainville Peace Process,* Conciliation Resources, London:n.p. Available online at http://www.c-r.org/accord/boug/accord12/from.shtml.

Ogan, E., 1990. 'Perspectives on a Crisis (5)', in P. Polomka (ed.), *Bougainville: perspectives on a crisis,* Strategic and Defence Studies Centre, Research School of Pacific Studies, Australian National University, Canberra:35–39.

——, 1999. *The Bougainville Conflict: perspectives from Nasioi*, State, Society and Governance in Melanesia Project Discussion Paper 99/3, Research School of Pacific and Asian Studies, The Australian National University, Canberra.

Oliver, D., 1991. *Black Islanders: a personal perspective of Bougainville 1937–1991*, Hyland House Publishing, Melbourne.

Ona, F., 1990. 'Perspectives on a crisis (1)', in P. Polomka (ed.), *Bougainville: Perspectives on a Crisis*, Strategic and Defence Studies Centre, Research School of Pacific Studies, Australian National University, Canberra:7–12).

Patrick, S., 2000. 'The donor community and the challenge of post-conflict recovery', in S. Forman and S. Patrick (eds), *Good Intentions: pledges of aid for post-conflict recovery*, Lynne Reinner, London:35–65.

Regan, A., 1998. 'Current developments in the Pacific', *The Journal of Pacific History*, 33(3):269–84.

——, 2001a. 'Why a neutral peace monitoring force? Tthe Bougainville conflict and the peace process', in M. Wehner and D. Denoon (eds), *Without a Gun: Australians' experiences monitoring peace in Bougainville, 1997–2001*, Pandanus Books and the Research School of Pacific and Asian Studies, The Australian National University, Canberra:2–18.

——, 2001b. 'Establishing the Truce Monitoring Group and Peace Monitoring Group', in M. Wehner and D. Denoon (eds), *Without a Gun: Australians' experiences monitoring peace in Bougainville, 1997-2001*, Pandanus Books and the Research School of Pacific and Asian Studies, The Australian National University, Canberra:21–41.

——, 2002a. 'Phases of the negotiation process', in A. Carl and L. Garasu (eds), *Weaving Consensus: the PNG–Bougainville Peace Process*, Conciliation Resources, London:n.p. Available online at http://www.c-r.org/accord/boug/accord12/phases.shtml.

——, 2002b. 'Resolving two dimensions of conflict: the dynamics of consent, consensus and compromise', in A. Carl and L. Garasu (eds), *Weaving Consensus: the PNG–Bougainville Peace Process*, Conciliation Resources, London:n.p. Available online at http://

www.c-r.org/accord/boug/accord12/resolving.shtml.

Rigby, A., 2001. *Justice and Reconciliation: after the violence,* Lynne Reiner, Boulder.

Ropers, N., 2001. 'Enhancing the quality of NGO work in peacebuilding', in L. Reychler and T. Paffenholz (eds), *Peacebuilding: a field guide,* Lynne Rienner Publishers, Boulder and London:520–27.

Saffu, Y., 1992. 'The Bougainville crisis and politics in Papua New Guinea', *The Contemporary Pacific,* 4(2):325–43.

Saovana-Spriggs, R., 2000. 'Christianity and Women in Bougainville', in B. Douglas (ed.), *Women and Governance from the Grassroots in Melanesia,* State Society and Governance in Melanesia Project, Research School of Pacific and Asian Studies, The Australian National University, Canberra: 29–32.

——, 2003. 'Bougainville women's role in conflict resolution in the Bougainville peace process', in S. Dinnen (ed.), *A Kind of Mending: restorative justice in the Pacific islands,* Pandanus Books, Canberra:195–213.

Scott, T.J., 2001. 'Evaluating development-oriented NGOs', in Claude E. Welch Jr. (ed.), *NGOs and Human Rights: promise and performance,* University of Pennsylvania Press, Philadelphia:204–21.

Sirivi, J., 1998. 'Surviving a nine year war', in de Ishtar (ed.), *Pacific Women Speak Out for Independence and Denuclearisation,* Raven Press, Christchurch:52–58.

—— and Havini, M., 2004. *As Mothers of the Land: the birth of the Bougainville women for peace and freedom,* Pandanus Books, Canberra.

Smillie, I., 1995. *The Alms Bazaar: altruism under fire—non profit organisations and international development,* IDRC, Ottawa.

Sogge, D., 2002. *Give and Take: what's the matter with foreign aid?,* Zed Books, London.

Spriggs, M., 1992. 'Alternative prehistories for Bougainville: regional, national and micronational', *The Contemporary Pacific,* 4(2):269–98.

Sohia, P., 2002. 'Early interventions', in A. Carl and L. Garasu (eds), *Weaving Consensus: the PNG–Bougainville Peace Process,* Accord

12, Conciliation Resources, London:n.p. Available online at http://www.c-r.org/accord/boug/accord12/early.shtml.

Spence, R., 1999. 'The centrality of community-led recovery', in G. Harris (ed), *Recovery from Armed Conflict in Developing Countries: an economic and political analysis*, Routledge, London:204–22.

Stokke, O. (ed), 1995. 'Aid and political conditionality: core issues and state of the art', in O. Stokke (ed), *Aid and Political Conditionality*, Frank Cass, London:1–87.

Tapi, R., 2002. 'From Burnham to Buin: sowing the seeds of peace in the land of the snow-capped mountains', in A. Carl and L. Garasu (eds), *Weaving Consensus: the PNG–Bougainville Peace Process*, Conciliation Resources, London:n.p. Available online at http://www.c-r.org/accord/boug/accord12/from.shtml.

Tong, R.P., 1998. *Feminist Thought*, 2nd edition, Westview Press, Boulder.

Tonissen, M., 2001. Violence against Women and Development in Post-conflict Bougainville, MA Thesis, University of Melbourne, Melbourne.

Tvedt, T., 1998. *Angels of Mercy or Development Diplomats? NGOs and foreign aid*, African World Press, Trenton.

UNESCO, 2000. *Developing Partner Cooperation in Support of Education For All: rationale and strategies*, Discussion Paper, UNESCO, Paris.

Van Tuijl, P., 1999. 'NGOs and human rights: sources of justice and democracy', *Journal of International Affairs*, 52(2):493–512.

——, 2000. 'Entering the global dealing room: reflections on a rights-based framework for NGOs in international development', *Third World Quarterly*, 21(4):617–26.

Wanyeki, L.M., 2004. 'Globalization and poverty in Africa', *Development*, 47(1):94–96.

Wasserman, S. and Pattison, P., 2004. 'Network analysis', in M.S. Lewis-Beck, A. Bryman and T. Futing Liao (eds), *The Sage Encyclopedia of Social Science Research Methods*, Sage, Thousand Oaks, California:719–25.

Weeks, A., 1994. 'Bougainville demands peace', *Peace Research*, 7(4):25–29.

Wesley-Smith, T. & Ogan, E., 1992. 'Copper, class and crisis: changing relations of production in Bougainville', *The Contemporary Pacific*, 4(2):245–67.

Yongo-Bure, B., 2003. 'NGOs and grassroots development in Sudan', *Journal of Development Alternatives and Area Studies*, 22(3/4):57–78.

INDEX

www.ingramcontent.com/pod-product-compliance
Lightning Source LLC
Chambersburg PA
CBHW050810270326
41926CB00049B/4646